M.B. F.V. Dickins

Hyak Nin Is'Shiu

M.B. F.V. Dickins

Hyak Nin Is'Shiu

ISBN/EAN: 9783741173301

Manufactured in Europe, USA, Canada, Australia, Japa

Cover: Foto ©Andreas Hilbeck / pixelio.de

Manufactured and distributed by brebook publishing software (www.brebook.com)

M.B. F.V. Dickins

Hyak Nin Is'Shiu

百人一首
HYAK NIN IS'SHIU,

OR

STANZAS BY A CENTURY OF POETS,

BEING

JAPANESE LYRICAL ODES,

TRANSLATED INTO ENGLISH, WITH EXPLANATORY NOTES,
THE TEXT IN JAPANESE AND ROMAN CHARACTERS,
AND A FULL INDEX.

BY

F. V. DICKINS, M.B.

"... cantina non prius
Audita canto."—Hor.

LONDON:
SMITH, ELDER, & CO., 65, CORNHILL.

1866.

PATRI MATRIQUE

CARISSIMIS

VERSIONEM HANC

CARMINUM ANTIQUORUM JAPONENSIUM

DICAT

DEDICAT

FILIUS AUCTOR

PREFACE.

The Odes of which I have endeavoured in the following pages to give an English rendering are familiar in every Japanese household, high and low, and every Japanese child has his memory stored with, at least, some of them. But few even among tolerably well-educated persons can understand perfectly the ancient dialect in which these Odes are written, or explain the allusions contained in them, and hence has arisen a crowd of commentaries, among which much notable difference of opinion is to be met with. I have followed the text given in the **Hyak Nin Is'-shiu Mine no Kakehashi**, or 'Steps to the Summit of the Hundred Odes of a Hundred Poets,'* which has appeared to me to be the fullest and most reliable of all the explanatory works on the subject that I have seen, and I have given short accounts of the allusions contained in the Odes, and of the authors of these, taken from the

---

* As we may, *Gradus ad Parnassum &c.*

above work. I have also added an Appendix, containing the original text, accompanied by some grammatical notes, intended chiefly to explain the word-plays so common in the Odes, and a vocabulary for the benefit of students of Japanese.

I do not pretend in all cases to have rendered the original with exactitude. For, differences of language and idiom, my imperfect acquaintance with many allusions, and, doubtless, imperfect appreciation of many metaphorical expressions, have compelled me sometimes to resort to a mere imitation where necessarily much of the force of the original disappears. Again, the helps to a thorough comprehension of the language are very few and very imperfect, and the reading of the various commentaries was very laborious, and too often with but little profit, because of the discrepancies of the explanations therein given. I must therefore ask for the indulgence of my readers, and especially of those among them who may have made a special study of the Japanese language, and who will doubtless detect errors and discrepancies in the following pages.

The Odes are all of a peaceful character, some didactic, some descriptive, and many amatory. Very often the point of the ode lies in a play upon

PREFACE

words, very telling in the original, but seldom capable of adequate rendering into English. The most ancient of them seem to have an antiquity of one thousand years, and the most modern of at least six hundred. Each ode has, on an average, thirty characters or syllables; sometimes one or two more when the sounds of these combine with the sounds of adjacent characters; and nothing in the nature of rhyme can be detected in them. They are always read in a somewhat monotonous singing falsetto, with scarcely any accentuation or emphasis, being, as it were, a mere slow recapitulation of the syllables composing them.

They are written in the old Yamato language, free from any intermixture of Chinese derivatives, a very noble and harmonious tongue, but much disfigured now by the introduction of such ill-sounding Sinico-Japanese syllables as rets', bats', mats', kats', shuts', and the like.

The compilation of the **Hyak Nin Is'-shiu** was the work of Teika or Sadaihe (refer to Ode 97), and was completed on the 27th day of the 5th month of the 2nd year of the "nengo" **Bun-reki** 文歷. Teika was a "kuge" living near Mount Ogura in Yamashiro, and was a contemporary of the celebrated poet

Motogori. The Hyak Nin Is'-shiu Mins no Kake-hash is the work of a man of letters, named Koromo-gawa-daijin, and was published at Kioto and Ohosaka. There are three prefaces: the first, dated 8th day of 3rd month of 3rd year of Bun-k'wa (A.D. 1805); the second, by a man of Inaba, spring of the 2nd year of Bun-k'wa (A.D. 1805); the third, by Motoi Ohoira, without any date. We find also at the end of the second and last volume of the work a postface, but equally devoid of date and of interest.

The Odes are taken from various sources, and were at first inserted in the Mei-gets-ki 明月記 'Records of Illustrious Months;' also a compilation of Teika's; but were afterwards separated, and were finally delivered into the care of Ten-kei, a priest of the temple of Naka no In, near the capital Kioto.

Finally, I would remind the reader, that the Odes of which the following translation is offered in no way lay claim to any high poetic merit, and are but prettily and somewhat cleverly-rendered metrical expressions of pretty but ordinary sentiments. But, whatever their intrinsic value may be, they are extremely popular with the Japanese, and on that account, rather than for any literary merit they may

PREFACE.

possess, have I ventured to offer this English version of them to the public.

It was found impossible to adopt a uniform metre, for, while some stanzas were complete (as to their meaning) in themselves, and could be rendered almost literally, others were suggestive of much more than what was verbally expressed, and were, besides, so full of allusions and word-plays, that a literal version of these would have been quite unintelligible; and I found myself compelled to resort to an imitation of the original, in which more or less amplification was necessary to render even a small portion of the point and force, and to explain with any degree of clearness, the leading ideas (often very difficult to make out) of the Japanese stanza.

I must claim indulgence for any clerical errors or typographical faults, for the work has been prepared under very adverse circumstances, and, indeed, would never have seen the light but for the kind assistance and advice of Professor Summers, to whom also I am indebted for preparing the text in the original character, and to whom I here express my heartiest thanks.

LONDON, *November*, 1866.

JAPANESE ODES

(TRANSLATED FROM THE ORIGINAL).

———o———

I.—Ten-ji Ten-wo.*

My lowly hut is thatched with straw
 From fields where rice-sheaves frequent stand,
Now autumn's harvest well-nigh o'er,
 Collected by my toiling hand:
Through tatter'd roof the sky I view,
 My clothes are wet with falling dew.

---

* *Ten-wo* signifies "Emperor." Ten-ji (lit. *sapientia celestis*) was the son of To-mui ten-wo and the Princess Takara no Hime-miko, and died (lit. "became a god") in the *nengo Tenchi* (A.D. 671),* at the temple of Otu', in the province of Ohomi, and was buried at Yama-shina, in the province of Yamashiro. The ode is found in the *Ko-kin-shiu*, or "Collection of Pieces Ancient and Modern;" but Japanese writers doubt the fact of Ten-ji being the author thereof.

* Vide "Yei-dai nen-dai-ki."

II.—Ji-to Ten-wō.[a]

The pleasant spring hath passed away,
Now summer follows close, I ween,
And Ama's[b] secret summit[c] may
In all its grandeur now be seen;
Of yore the drying ground,
Whitened with angels' robes, spread far around.

III.—Kaki-no-moto no H'tomaro.[c]

The hill-side fowl his long-drooped tail
Sweeps o'er the ground—so drags the night.
My lonely plight
I mourn—my sleepless wretchedness bewail.

---

[a] Ji-to was the daughter of Ten-jī. Her mother was the daughter of Ishi-kawa-maro, a *daijin*, or nobleman of Saganoyamada. She married the Emperor Ten-mu, and after his death, in the 2nd year of *Dai-ho* (A.D. 702), assumed the government. The ode is extracted from the *Man-yo-shiu*, or "Collection of 10,000 Leaves," a miscellany of fugitive pieces.

[b] In the original *Ama-kagu yama*. The meaning of *kagu* is explained in the *Naru-bèshi*, a work treating on the ancient language of Japan, and on common errors and misapplications of words.

[c] Son of Ko-sho, the fifth *nin-wo*, or "human king," so called from a kaki-tree (*Diospyros kaki*), said to have overshadowed his birth-place. He is supposed to have become disgraced, because, in the *Man-yo-shiu*, the term *shiru* (used only with reference to persons of low

* In Milton we have "the secret top of Oreb."

IV.—Yamabe no Akah'to.^a

From where my home,—
　My lonely home,—on Tago's shore
Doth stand, the wandering eye may roam
O'er Fusiyama's summit hoar,
　Whose lofty brow
Is whitened by th' new-fallen snow.

V.—Saru-maru Ta-iu.^b

Now 'mid the hills the Momiji
　Is trampled down 'neath hoof of deer,
Whose plaintive cries continually
　Are heard both far and near;
　　My shivering frame
Now autumn's piercing chills doth blame.

---

rank) is employed to record his death. He is also called Kaki-no-moto no H'toshlu, *shiu* being equivalent to *maro*, the term of a rank among the *kuge*, or noblemen of the *Tenshi's* court, that, in the reign of *Ten-mu* (7th century of our era), was changed into *asen*.

^a Of whom nothing is known. In the *Man-yo-shiu* he is supposed to have flourished in the reign of Gen-sho (1), who became *Tenshi* in A.D. 715.

^b Of whom nothing is known. *Ta-iu* (2) is the appellation of a rank of the fifth order. The ode is found in the *Ko-kin-shiu*.

^c *Cerv dissectum.*

VI.—Chiu-nagon Yakamochi.[a]

Upon the bridge[b] where ravens, aye,
Do love to pass where hoar-frost's sheen,
When hoar-frost's glittering film is seen;
I trow the break of day is nigh.

---

[a] *Chiu-nagon* is a rank in the Mikado's court. Yakamochi was a great-grandson of a *mikoto*, or lord of Michinōomi, a *dai-nagon* of high rank, who flourished towards the end of the 8th century. In the *Honcho-bun-shiu* the following story is told of our author. His brothers, Otomonotsu and Takera, murdered a man, Tanetsugu, in the province of Oshiu. He is falsely implicated in the crime, and, with them, banished to an island; but his innocence being afterwards established through the agency of a friend, Tomonoyoshino, he is finally released, and a higher rank is bestowed upon him.

[b] The allusion is to a bridge in the imperial grounds, much resorted to by his majesty. The poet, availing himself of a word-play on the name of this bridge (at least, that seems to be the best explanation), insinuates a comparison between it and the famous Kasasagi-bash'. On *Tanabata* night (7th of 7th moon), the ravens *(kasasagi)* are supposed to fly towards the stars Shokujo[c] and Kengio,[c] and their long and densely-crowded line is said to form a bridge *(bash')* across the Amagawa river. The bridge of the *Tcushi* the poet contemplates with as much pleasure as if it were the latter-mentioned ideal bridge, for has he not contemplated it until nigh daybreak, as proved by his seeing the hoar-frost, which does not fall until very near morning !

[c] A goddess and god, from whose embraces resulted the "Amagawa," (3) or "milky-way." So in Grecian mythology we are told that it consisted of the droppings from Juno's breasts.

VII.—Abe no Nakamaro.[a]

On every side the vaulted sky
   I view: now will the moon have peered,
I trow, above Mikasa high
   In Kasuga's far-off land upreared.[b]

VIII.—Ki-sen Hoshi.[c]

My cabin doth in Tats'mi lie
   Miako's[d] city near,
Yo-uji men my mountain call,
   Yet still do I dwell here.

---

[a] Son of Funamori, a *kuge* of the rank of *Naka-tsukasa no ta-fu*. In the 8th month of the 2nd year of *Anki*(?), A.D. 716, he, with Agatamori and Kibi Daijin, visit China to investigate Chinese literature and civilization. Contrary winds detained him there, and it is said that he died in China. The *Nihon-gi* (5), "History of Japan," doubts his being the son of Funamori.

[b] Detained away from his own country, the author laments how that he cannot view the moon, which at this time will be rising above the well-known ridge of Mikasa yama.

[c] Said to have been a son of Tachi-bana-naru-maru.

[d] Miako is the metropolis. The neighbouring district is divided into portions named after the signs of the Zodiac, among which are *Tats-mi*, "dragon-serpent." The ode is found in the *Ko-kin-shiu*.

IX.—Onono-ko-machi.*

Thy love hath passed away from me
Left desolate, forlorn—
In winter-rains how wearily
The summer past I mourn!

X.—Semi maro.^b

Some hence towards the city haste,
Some from the city here speed by,
Here friends and strangers meet and part,
With kindly glance and careless eye;
Apt is the name it seems to me,
Ausaka gate, men give to thee.^c

---

* In *Sei-shi-roku-hon* said to be sister of Dai-toku-ono, of whom nothing certain is recorded. In conjunction with Ono-tei-jin (probably a male relation), she is supposed to have composed many other odes found as the above in the *Ko-kin-shiu*. The book *Go-sen-shiu* mentions her in connection with a *kenjo*, of the temple of Ishiyama, and, as this was a very ancient priestly rank, existent for a short time only after the introduction of Buddhism, she may have flourished about the reign of Bun-toku (6), in the early part of the 9th century.

^b In *Kin-seki-monogatari* (7), "Relation of Events Ancient and Modern," he is supposed to be the son of Uda ten-wo, who flourished about A.D. 882. Becoming blind, he was incapable of succeeding to the throne, and he buried himself in a lonely hut, built beside an *ausaka* or mountain-path, close to a barrier-gate, where he endeavoured to while away the hours with playing on the *biha* (a sort of banjo-like musical instrument—the Chinese *pipa*, "guitar.")

^c The point of the piece lies in a *jeu de mot* on the word *ausaka*, which means "a mountain pass or path," and which also may signify

XI.—Sangi Takamura.[*]

Ye fishermen, who range the sea
In many a barque, I pray ye tell
My fellow-villagers of me—
How that far o'er vast ocean's swell.
In vessel frail
Towards Yasoshima I sail.

"a place of meeting," wherefore the author praises the aptness of the term *awauka no seki* applied to the barrier-gate sometimes erected across mountain roads, for here meet those who are journeying to or from the capital, here meet and part those who are acquainted and those who are unacquainted with each other.

[*] His entire title is Sangi-sadai-hen-jiu-san-i-onono-ason Takamura. According to *Bun-toku-jiu-roku-hon*, he died in the 2nd year of *Nin-jiu* (8) (A.D. 852). His father was Sangi-sashi-nogi Mine no Kami. Takamura, originally very poor, became rich, as supervisor of ships coming from China. Reported by envious people to the Tenshi as a robber and embezzler, he is banished to the *Yasoshima*, "eighty isles," near Oki, on the west coast of Nippon, on which occasion he indited his song to a friend. The Tenshi afterwards learns the innocence of the slandered Takamura, and restores him to his former rank.

XII.—So-jo Hen-jo.[a]

In fitful path across the sky,
By various winds of heaven forced,
Cloud-borne Otome glideth by—
Now hath the breeze its vigour lost
An instant, and her form so bright
For a fleeting moment greets my sight.[b]

---

[a] In youth called Mune-sada. Son of a *kuge*, Yas'yoha. In his sorrow for the death of the Tenshi Bun-toku, he became a priest, and died in the 2nd year of *Kam-pei* (9), A.D. 890. He is said to have inflicted death upon himself, according to the custom called *Nin-motz*, which is briefly as follows:—The sufferer is placed in a small stone enclosure, and covered with earth, a small pipe conveying to his mouth sufficient air to breathe. Here he remains till he dies of hunger and exhaustion. It is a kind of voluntary self-sacrifice even now, it is said, occasionally undergone in remembrance of a much-loved lord, for whom the sufferer prays incessantly until death. [This custom is the modified form of that ancient usage of burying the servants of a king or prince with their deceased master, mentioned in Herodotus and Japanese history.—J. S.]

[b] *Literally*.—"The winds of Heaven" cause the clouds to drift onwards lightly ; if there be a lull, the form of Otome (a goddess) will linger for an instant in sight." [The poet, at a dancing-feast on one of the *Go-sek-ku*[c] days, compares the motion of the dancing-girl to the fitful course of the cloud-borne goddess, Otome.]

[c] "Go-sek-ku" are five feast days—1st of 1st month, 3rd of 3rd month, 5th of 5th month, 7th of 7th month, 9th of 9th month. The "odd" is supposed to be the male or highest of the duals "odd and even," whence the choice of these days. The 11th month is not included, because 10 represents completion with the Jap. and Chin. philosophers.

XIII.—Yo-sei In.[a]

The Minagawa's waters fall
 From Tsukubaneyama's lofty peak:
In loving haste the waters all
 For aye accumulate, and seek
  The end of all their constant flow,
  The sea that doth no limits know.[b]

XIV.—Kawara no Sadai-jin.[c]

Ah me! my soul with cares is vext,
Unnumbered, crowded, and perplext,
Than varied pattern more confus'd
On Mojidsuri[d] fabric used,
 The produce of Shinobu's loom,
 Shinobu in Michinoku land;
 For whose sake whose but thine doth gloom
 Hold o'er my failing heart command.

---

[a] Yo-sei In was so called after death. In life, Yo-sei Ten-wo. His name in youth was Sata-akira. His father was Sei-wa Ten-wo, his mother Queen Takai-ko, of Nijo, a place near Kioto. He became Tenshi A.D. 877, abdicated A.D. 884, and died in the 3rd year of Tenryak (10), A.D. 949, according to the Nen-dai-ki, above quoted.

[b] This ode is addressed to the Princess Tsuridono no miko, to whom the poet thus insinuates that his love for her, increasing day by day, accumulating as the waters of the waterfall, has at last become immeasurable in extent.

[c] Son of Sago Ten-wo and his kiaki, or queen, a daughter of the house of Ohohara. Died A.D. 895.

[d] Mojidsuri is a silk fabric embroidered with intricate designs of

XV.—Kwo-ko Ten-wo.[a]

Thy wishes, love, have I obeyed,
And 'mid the meadows have I strayed
In this spring-time, and sought with care
The wakana[b] plant that groweth there.
    Lo on my sleeve
The falling snow its trace doth leave.[c]

XVI.—Chiu-nagon Yuki-hira.[d]

Inaba's lofty range is crowned
By many a tall pine-tree;
Ah quickly were I homewards bound
If thou shouldst pine for me.[e]

---

flowers, &c. Found in the *Ko-kin-shiu*, and addressed to the author's *kimi*, or mistress. The above translation is necessarily an amplification of the original, so far as words are concerned, but no new idea has been introduced.

[a] Son of Niu-mei Ten-wo and the daughter of Fuji-waro-notsuna-t'sne, a *daijōo daijin*. In early life his name was Toki-yasu'. He became Tenshi in the 8th year of *Gen-kei* (11), A.D. 834.

[b] *Wakana* is an eatable vegetable. In Chinese, *Tung-fung-tsai* (12), or "east-wind vegetable," the young *Brassica Orientalis*, that becomes eatable about the new year, when east-winds are common.

[c] The poet had gathered the *wakana* to please his mistress, and takes credit for having gone out in the cold to do so, in proof of which he shows the snow on his dress.

[d] Son of Heijo Ten-wo. In the reign of Yo Sei (Ode 13), became a *chiu-nagon*, and died 853 A.D. Found in *Ko-kin-shiu*.

[e] A close translation is impossible, and the above pretends only to be

XVII.—Ariwara no Narihira-ason.[a]

O Tatsta! when th' autumnal flow
I watch of thy deep, ruddy wave—
E'en when the stern gods long ago
Did rule, was ne'er beheld so brave,
So fair a stream as thine, I vow.

XVIII.—Fujiwara no Toshiyuki-ason.[b]

Tho' softly as the waves do break
On Suminoye's shore, I seek
To meet thee, love e'en in a dream,
To dread men's curious eyes I seem.

an imitation—of the original:—Yuki-hira leaves his wife to go to Inaba, and endeavours to soothe, by the above lines, her sorrow at his departure. The point of the stanza lies in the word-play on "mats" (see Appendix). In a former translation, a different but equally possible rendering is given. Below is the original pointed according to the two ways of explaining its sense:—1. Tachi-ware, Inaba no yama no mine no ōrū; mats to shi kikaba ima kaherikon. 2. Tachi-wakare Inaba no yama no mine ni ōrū mats (to lō koto) to shi kikaba. ima kaherikon. It is also possible that a word-play is intended on "toshi," "toshi" (p. xiv.), or "to shi" (18), but that I leave to the consideration of students of Japanese.

[a] Son of Yukih'ra (Ode 16) and the Princess Ita'no Hime-miko. According to the *San-dai-jits-toku-kon*, he was the son of Awo Shin-wō and the daughter of Kammu Ten-wo, and died in the 4th year of *Gen-kei* (A. D. 880). He is said to have composed the song upon seeing a representation of the river Tatsta on a *biōbu*, or screen, in the apartments of Haru-mia, the *kinshi* (vid. Ode 13) of Nijō. The Japanese poets are never tired of praising the autumn, the fall of the leaf, and reddening of the waters of the streams, the various tints of the woods, and other autumnal beauties.

[b] Son of Azechi fuji-mara. According to the *San-dai-jits-toku-kon*,

XIX.—Ise.[a]

Scant are the joints of Ashi reed
That grow Nanihagata[b] nigh,
While time o'er e'en as brief space speed
Failst thou to greet my longing eye.
I fain would die![c]

XX.—Motoyoshi Shin-wo.[d]

Distracted by my misery,
How utterly forlorn am I;
Oh that I might thee once more see,
Tho' it should cost my life to me!

---

in the 2nd year of *Nin-wa* (A.D. 886), he was invested with the rank of *Kon-ye-no-sosho*. According to the *Ko-kin-shiu*, during *Kam-pei* (889-897), the courtiers were assembled by order of the Tenshi, to whom each one presented a poem of his own composition. And on this occasion Fujiwara presented the above.

[a] A Princess, daughter of Fujiwara no Tsugu-kane, Lord of Ise, placed at the court of the Emperor Kwo-ko, in the 2nd year of *Nin-wa* (14), A.D. 886.

[b] Near Ohosaka.

[c] She means, she would rather die than not see her lover, were it only for a brief visit.

[d] *Shin-wo* is a title of the heir-apparent of the Tenshi. The author died in *Ten-kei* (15), A.D. 943.

XXI.—Sosei Hoshi.[a]

Oh, maiden! heedless of thy vow,
 Why com'st thou not? 'Tis "long-moon" night,
And th' Ariake moon shines now,
 Forgetfulless with welcome light.[b]

XXII.—Bunya no Yasuhide.[c]

Now autumn's gales, in various freak,
 On herb, on tree, destruction wreak,
And wildest roar
 The gusts that down from Mube[d] pour.

---

[a] Son of So-jo hen-jo, born before the latter became a priest (about A.D. 850). Vide Yamato-monogatari, or "Relation of Events in Yamato."

[b] Why is not the maid as faithful to her promise as the moon to her duty?

[c] Said to have been the great-grandson of Naga no Shin-wo and son of Ten-mu Ten-wo. According to the Ko-kin-shiu, he was a kuge of the country of Mika. Flourished in the 9th century. The poem was composed at a meeting of kuge in the palace of Kore-sado Shin-wo,[e] held for the purpose of literary intercourse and poetic competition.

[d] Mube or Ube is a mountain noted for the violent winds there met with.

[e] "Shin-wo" is the title of the brother of the reigning Tenshi, or heir-apparent.

XXIII.—Ohoye no Chisato.

How oft' my glance upon the moon hath dwelt,
Her secret power my soul subdued—
Her sadd'ning influence I alone have felt,
Though all men autumn's moon have viewed.

XXIV.—Kan-ke.

This time, I ween, no need there be,
A nusa^b I should take with me:
The nishki of the maple-tree
Tamuke-yama thou dost show.
'Twill serve the gods full well, I trow.

---

^a The author complains that, though all men view the moon, they do not become saddened as he does when he contemplates her. In the *Ko-kin-shiu* we are told that the above stanza was composed at the instance and in the apartments of the wife of Kore-mda Shin-wo.

^b A nusa is an emblem or staff held in the hand during certain prayers. It is covered with an embroidered silk fabric called *nishki* (16). The point of the ode lies in this word *nishki*, which also means "autumnal tints." He will see the *momiji* (maples), with their autumn-red leaves (*nishki*), as he passes near Tamuke°-yama, and will not, therefore, need to take with him the *nishki*-covered nusa.

° For "Tamuke," see Appendix.

XXV.—Sanjo Udaijin.[a]

If thou'rt as fair as rumour thee
   Doth paint, O deign my hut to grace,
And may thy path as secret be
   To human eye as is the trace
     Of Sanakadz'ra[b] 'mid
     Osaka-yama's forests hid!

XXVI.—Tei-ah'n Ko.[c]

The redd'ning leaves of th' momiji
   That on Ogura's summit grow,
How pleasant 'tis their tints to see!
   Ah! did they but their beauty know,
     They would linger till there pass'd again
     Our Emperor's miyuki[d] train.

---

[a] Died in the 2nd year of Shō-hei (A.D. 932). According to the Go-ren-shiu, the person addressed and the motive of the ode are equally unknown.

[b] The sanakadz'ra (uvario japonica) is a slender creeper prostrate among the underwood, and not therefore easily seen. A mucilage extracted from this plant is used by women in dressing the hair, and also is employed in the manufacture of paper.

[c] The father of Tei-ah'n Ko was a nobleman of the name of Moto-tsune Ko, who died in the 3rd year of Ten-ryak (A.D. 949). He was a man of ability and valour, and on him was conferred the rank of Shō-ichi II. He is said to have accompanied Uda Ten-wo to Ohoigawa;[e] and at this period probably was the ode composed.

[d] Miyuki (17) is the appellation of a journey or progress made by the Tenshi, or Emperor.

[e] There is a stream "Ohoigawa" in Enshiu, but that is not the one here meant.

XXVII.—Chiu-nagon Kaneska.ᵃ

Lo Idsmi's boiling waters flow,
    With tumult vast, through Mika's plain;
My mind doth like confusion know,
    A wretched prey to lover's pain.ᵇ

XXVIII.—Minamoto Mineyuki-ason.ᶜ

The hamlet bosom'd 'mid the hills
    Aye lonely is; in winter-time
Its solitude with mis'ry fills
    My mind, for now the rig'rous clime
        Hath banished every herb and tree
        And every human face from me.

ᵃ Son of Sachiū ahō Toshimoto. Died in the 3rd year of *Shō-hei* (A.D. 933). The ode is found in the *Ko-kin-shiu*.

ᵇ The motive of the above ode is not clear. Probably, the author thereof refers to the doubtfulness of his seeing or hearing his mistress again.

ᶜ Son of Koretada Shin-wu, and grandson of the Emperor Ko-kwo. Died in the 3rd year of *Ten-kei* (15). A.D. 940. The ode is found in the *Ko-kin-shiu*.

XXIX.—Ohoshi-ka-uchi no Mitsune.

I had to pluck thee, flower,—thought—
To pluck thee, flower, in vain I sought:
The earliest hoar-frost feigning thee,
Fair Shiragiku,[a] cheated me.

XXX.—Mibu no Tadamine.

The 'Ariake-moonbeams will
In th' morning heaven linger still;
While I from thee—how hard the smart—
By Akudaki[b] compelled, must part.[c]

---

[a] The *shiragiku* is a kind of white chrysanthemum. The ode is from the *Ko-kin-shiu.*

[b] *Ariake* is a term applied to the moon when she shines throughout the night. *Akadaki* is "the dawn of day," when the lover must depart, while the envied moon still lingers in the sky, mingling her rays with the grey beams of the dawn.

[c] The lover is envious of *Ariake* moon, that may linger after the *Akadaki*, or dawn—in the sky—while he at *Akadaki* must not linger in his mistress's dwelling.

JAPANESE ODES.

XXXI.—Saka no uye no Korenori.

Now clearly broke the dawning day,
Ariake moon I thought to see—
The newly-fallen snow that lay
Round Yoshino[a] deceived me.
The whiten'd hill-side seemed
As tho' thereon the moonlight streamed.

XXXII.—Haru-michi no Tsuraki.[b]

The winds of autumn have amassed
Dried withered leaves in ruddy heaps,
Have them in th' mountain-torrent cast,
Whose stream in stony channel sweeps;
Amid the rocks that bar the way
The Mom-ji's reddened leaves delay.[c]

---

[a] Yoshino, otherwise Miyoshino, is a hill-village in Yamato. The ode is extracted from the Ko-kin-shiu.

[b] Son of Shoroku-i-no-jo Monobano Kadoki. Died in the 3rd year of Tei-k'wan (19), A.D. 864.

[c] The poet visits the wilds of Shigayama, and, on seeing the masses of dried and autumn-reddened maple-leaves entangled among the rocks of the mountain streams, composes the above stanza.

XXXIII.—Kino Tomo-nori.[a]

'Tis a pleasant day of merry spring,
No bitter frosts are threatening,
No storm-winds blow, no rain-clouds low'r,
　The sun shines bright on high,
Yet thou, poor trembling little flow'r,
　Dost wither away and die.[b]

XXXIV.—Fujiwara no Okikaze.[c]

Of old companions bereft,
　Men's friendship more I may not seek,
Nought but the ancient pine-trees left,
　That grow on Takasago's peak,
　　Comrades of many a year now gone,
　　But not the friends for whom I mourn.

---

[a] Grandson of Take no Uchisukune, a famous warrior in the early wars with Chōsen (Corea).

[b] The poet refers to the blossoms of the sakura (*prunus cerasus*), which wither about the end of spring.

[c] Son of Michinari. In the 11th year of Yen-ki (A.D. 911), we find him in an official position in the province of Sagami. The ode is extracted from the *Ko-kin-shiu*.

XXXV.—Ki no Tsurayuki.[a]

The comrades of my early days
  Their former friend indifferent view,
Who with a wondering eye doth gaze
  On th' village that of old he knew
So well. O flower! thy fragrancy
Alone familiar seems to me.

XXXVI.—Kyowara no Fukayabu.[b]

Twas a summer's night, I scarcely thought
  The evening hours had passed away
When dawn broke; long the moon I'd sought,
  Nor knew where 'mid the clouds she lay.

---

[a] Flourished about the middle of the 10th century. Returning, after long absence, to his native village, he finds that no one recognises him, and everything appears strange. But the fragrancy of the wild cherry (sakura) has not altered, and is still familiar to him. The ode is from the Ko-kin-shiu.

[b] According to Seishiroh' (20), "Catalogue of Family Names," grandson of Bitats Ten-wo; in Oho-koi-dzu (21), "Complete Panorama of Families," of Toneri Shin-wo; in San-dai-jitz'-roku (22), "True Catalogue of the Three Dynasties," son of Kyowara no Mahito.

[c] The night was so short, that the dawn broke unawares upon the poet, who had been contemplating the moon. The ode is from the Ko-kin-shiu.

XXXVII.—Bunya no Asayasu.ᵃ

Now dew-drops sparkling o'er the moor are seen,
　The autumn gust sweeps howling by,
Scarce lurks an instant 'mid the reeds I ween:
　In timid show'r the dew-drops fly,
　And, scattered o'er the grass, there lie.ᵇ

XXXVIII.—Ukon.ᶜ

A solemn oath thou swor'st with me,
I dreamt thou wouldest constant be—
Forgotten, scorned, the penalty
Of death I almost cry on thee.

ᵃ Son of Bunya no Yasuhide.

ᵇ The above ode was composed at the request of the Emperor Daigo, in Yen-ki (A. D. 900).

ᶜ Daughter of Suyenawa-shosho, according to the Yamato-monogatari. Wife of the Emperor Koguu, who is supposed to have deserted her for the charms of another. But in the Jiu-i-shiu we are told that the motive of the poem is unknown.

XXXIX.—Sangi Hitoshi.[a]

Like humble Asajiu[b] amid
The reeds of Ono's moor hid,
 I would my passion were concealed
But by its flower the Asajiu:
By my too ardent love for you
 My secret passion stands revealed.[c]

XL.—Taira no Kanemori.

Tho' aye I strive my lot to hide,
My face to all the secret tells:
My changing visage, sorely tried,
 Shows that deep passion in me dwells:
And all men ask,
What griefs my altered features task![d]

---

[a] The father of Sangi Hitoshi died in the 3rd year of *Ten-ryak* (23).

[b] The *asajiu* is a plant that bears a conspicuous florescence. Another name for it is *tsubana*.

[c] The above ode is an address to the author's mistress. From the *Go-sen-shiu*.

[d] From the *Riu-i-shiu* (24), where the ode is said to have been composed at the instance of the Tenshi Daigo, in *Ten-ryak* (A.D.) 949.

XLI.—Mibu no Tadami.[a]

My love for thee of every tongue
　The daily theme is—far and wide
My name is bruited men among.
　Ah me! my heart was sorely tried
　　With no unfounded fears, lest
　My love to all should stand confest.

XLII.—Kyewara no Motosuke.[b]

When last each other we embraced,
　A solemn vow of faith we swore,
And sealed it with the tears that chased
Adown our cheeks our drench'd sleeves o'er—
　　That we our oath would fail to keep
When th' waves o'erleapt S'ye's pine-crown'd steep.[c]

---

[a] Son of Mibu no Tadamine. The ode was composed on the occasion referred to in the note to Ode 40.

[b] Son of Fuka-yabu. Died 1st year of Fei-so (25). Found in the Go-sen-shiu.

[c] Reference to a proverb common in Michinoku:—To keep a vow while the waves do not overleap Suyematz-yama is to keep a vow for ever. The negative form here used is that of original.

XLIII.—Chiu-nagon Atsutada.[a]

I went to meet thee, dearest maid,
   And when I parted loth from thee,
Upon my soul such mis'ry weighed,
   I mourned the love that burdened me:
     O that my heart
     Were still unvexed by lover's smart!

XLIV.—Chiu-nagon Asatada.[b]

To love, were it not human fate,
   Then men their fellows would not shun,
Their very selves they would not hate,
   As since love's birth they've ever done.

---

[a] Son of Honjiu no Sadaijin. Died, according to the *Jiu-i-shiu*, in the 6th year of *Ten-kei*.

[b] Son of an *Udaijin*, *Sadakata*. Died in the 5th year of *Ten-toku*[c] (25), A.D. 961. Composed, according to the *Jiu-i-shiu*, at the instance of the Emperor Daigo,, in *Ten-ryak* (A.D. 961).

[c] According to the "Hei-dai-nen-dai-ki," there are only four years in the "nengo Ten-toku."

XLV.—Ken-toku Ko.[a]

Ah, cruel one! thou pass'dst me by,
  No glance of pity on me turned,
A careless scorn was in thine eye,
  That mock'd the passion that in me burn'd:
    Alas! alas!
  Such woes my failing pow'rs surpass.

XLVI.—Sone no Yoshitada.[b]

The fishers' barques in safety glide
  O'er th' broad expanse of Yura's bay,
Their rudder lost o'er Yura's tide,
  In vague uncertain path they stray:
    The course of love doth, too,
  A like uncertain path pursue.

[a] Died in the 3rd year of *Ten-roku* (A.D. 972). The ode is extracted from the *Jiu-i-shiu*.

[b] Nothing known of him. The ode is from the *Shin-ko-kin-shiu*.

XLVII.—Yekue Hoshi.

My mountain dwelling's roof of thatch
Is with Yahemugura moss o'ergrown,
Of passer-by no glimpse I catch,
I dwell uncheered and alone;
    'Tis autumn time,
And mankind dread the rig'rous clime.[a]

XLVIII.—Minamoto no Shigeyuki.[b]

From th' pitiless rock are backwards flung
The wind urged floods in scattered spray.
With prayers from anguished heart-depths wrung,
I seek to make thee, love, obey;
    As spurns the rock
The waves, dost thou my passion mock.

---

[a] According to the *Jiu-i-shiu*, the above ode is a lament on the ragged and dilapidated condition of the temple of *Kawara In*, of which the author was priest.

[b] Father Jigo-I-nogo Kanenobu died in the province of Oshiu, in the nengo *As-wa* (A.D. 963). The ode was composed at the instance of Reisen In.*

* "In" is an appellation often given to the Tenshi after death.

XLIX.—Ohonakatomi[a] Yoshinobu-ason.

Th' Mikaki-mori through the night
  (And men the warder Yeji name)
The watch-fire's blaze keeps full and bright;
  When morning breaks, then dies the flame:
    So, too, at dawn
    My happiness is past and gone.

L.—Fujiwara no Yoshitaka.[b]

Ere I, O maid! had worshipped thee,
  A drear, uncared-for life was mine:—
O may long years be granted me
  Now that my heart, O maid, is thine!

---

[a] *Ohonakatomi* is the name of the rank of certain officers charged with religious duties. The author was a son of Yori-moto no Ason, and flourished in the reign of Bummu (27). The ode is from the *Sai ka-shiu* (28), or "Poetical Anthology."

[b] Died in the 2nd year of Ten-yen (29), A.D. 974. Found in the *Jiu-i-shiu*.

LI.—Mother of Udai-shō Michi-tsuna.[a]

I have watched weeping through the night,
    Deserted, desolate, alone,
Till now hath broke the morning light
I almost deemed for ever gone,
        So slowly by
    The creeping hours seemed to his.[b]

LII.—Mother of Gi-do-san-shi.[c]

To keep the vows that lovers swear
Of faithfulness and constancy
Through life till death and worldly care,
O'ertasketh human frailty,
        I trow. To-day
    I'd fain my spirit fled away.

---

[a] Daughter of Fujiwara no Motoyas', wife of Higashi-san-jō-sess'-shō Kane-ihē-kō, authoress of the *Sei-rei-nik'ki* (30), "Daily Jottings in the Land having the Similitude of a Dragon-fly," *i.e.* in Japan, a miscellany of poetic fugitive pieces.

[b] The husband coming home late, has to wait some time at the gate of his house before he can rouse the sleepy porter to let him in. He is very angry at this, and begins to reproach his wife, who turns round upon him with the above complaint.

[c] Wife of Naka no kambaku Michi-taka-ko. Flourished about 1001. The ode is from the *Ko-kin-shiu*. Jealousy of her husband is supposed to be the motive of the piece.

LIII.—Fujiwara no Sane-kata-ason.[a]

To tell thee of my love were vain,
  Its depth to me is scarcely known:
As writhes the flesh 'neath Moxa's pain,
  The Moxa on Ibuki grown,
    So madly writhes my spirit 'mong
Love's flames, ere now unknown, sore wrung.

LIV.—Fujiwara no Michinobu-ason.[b]

When day breaks, tho' full well I know
  The darkness of the ensuing night
The hated day shall overthrow:
  Yet aye the daylight do I hate,
    And bitterly mourn
Th' unwelcome breaking of the dawn.[c]

---

[a] Little known of the author. The ode is from the *Jiu-i-shiu*.

[b] Son of T'sunenori-ko, and adopted son of Michikaneko.

[c] The poet laments that the dawn separates him from his mistress, even though he knows that the day will be followed again by the more welcome night, when he will once more meet her. The ode is from the *Jiu-i-shiu*.

LV.—Dai-nagon Kin-tau.^a

The noisy play of the waterfall
 Hath ceased long ago,
Yet aye shall men its fame recall,
 Tho' none now list its flow.^b

LVI.—Ids'mi Sh'kibu.^c

Ere long for me this world shall end,
 Thus doth my mind to me foretell;
Ere long to other world shall wend
 My soul that thee hath lov'd so well.
  Ah! would that thou
  But once more wer't beside me now.^d

---

^a Died in the 2nd year of *Chō-kiu* (31), A.D. 1041.

^b An address to a waterfall in the grounds of the celebrated temple of Daikaku in Saga. The ode is from the *Jiu-i-shiu*.

^c Daughter of Ohoye no Masatoki, wife of Yas'masa, Lord of Tamba.

^d She was ill, and nigh upon death, when she addressed this ode to her absent lover (some say husband). The ode is from the *Jiu-i-shiu*.

LVII.—Murasaki Shikibu.[a]

I ventured forth one moonlight night,
And then saw some one hastening past,
Ere I could tell who 'twas aright,
With dark clouds was the moon o'ercast,
　　Whose pallid ray
O'er th' middle night held tranquil sway.[b]

LVIII.—Dai-ni no Sammi.[c]

More fickle thou than th' winds that pour
Down Arima o'er Ina's moor,
And still my love for thee as yet
I have forgotten to forget.[d]

---

[a] Daughter of Ji-go-i-no-ge Fujiwara no Tametoki, celebrated as the authoress of *Gen-ji Monogatari*, a collection of histories 54 in number, to each of which is prefixed a figure composed of five upright strokes, variously connected by horizontal ones, thus—

                                                &c., &c.,

and to these names are given which serve to designate the stories.

[b] She had gone to meet her lover, but the sudden darkening of the moon prevented her from finding him. The ode is from the *Ko-kin-shū*, where it is explained that, even though she did not meet him, her fair fame was darkened from that instant, like unto the moon, just then suddenly concealed by the clouds.

[c] Daughter of Fujiwara no Nobutaka. Wife of Dai-ni Nariakira.

[d] An address to a faithless lover. The ode is from the *Jiu-i-shiu*.

LIX.—Aka-some Yemon.[a]

I wait thy coming, love—repose
    Veils not mine eyes—far in the night
I watch the moon till nigh the close
    Of her celestial path of light.[b]

LX.—Koshikibu no Naishi.[c]

The road that crosseth o'er the plain
    Towards Ikuno 's full long for thee,
The road that far away doth gain
    The distant range of Ohoye:
        At Ama-no-hashi-date e'en
        Thy footsteps yet hath no one seen.

---

[a] Daughter of Toki-mochi, Lord of Yamato, wife of Masaf'sa. Flourished in the reign of the Emperor Ten-mu, about the middle of the 7th century.

[b] Addressed to the Kambuku, Michitaka-kyo, a kugé of high rank, apparently disdainful of the authoress' love. The ode is from the Jiu-i-shiu.

[c] Daughter of Tachibana no Michisada, Lord of Idzumi, and his wife, Idzumi-sh'kibu (date unknown). Her mother, after the death of Michisada, married Yasumasa, and lived in Tango. She was celebrated for her poetic talent, and her daughter, too, enjoyed much poetic power. On some of the verses of this latter being read at the court, people refused to believe that they were the composition of the daughter, and averred that they were written by the mother, on hearing which Koshkibu replies as above. At Amanohashidate (probably somewhere between the place of her mother's residence and her own) her mother has never been, nor has her mother's handwriting (vide Appendix) ever been seen there, so that it is not possible that any aid from that quarter should have been afforded her. Ikuno, Ohoye, and Amanohashidate are all places in Tango.

LXI.—Ise no Chouka.^a

Of old the Yahemak'ra lent
 To Nara,^b capital of yore,
Its fragrancy, and now its scent
 Hath spread our Kokonohe^c o'er.

LXII.—Sei Sho-nagon.

Tho' thou, the guardians of the gate
Of Kan-kok'-kan, with false cock-crow,
Might'st cheat, and thus anticipate
The morn, thou ne'er canst cheat, I trow,
Ausaka's gate, that thee
Shall keep until the morning be.^d

---

^a Wife of Takahash'nari-jun, Lord of Chik'zen. The ode is from the *Shi-ka-shiu*.

^b Nara, "Kokonohe, ancient capital cities. When the Emperor removed from the former to the latter, he took with him the *Yahemakura* trees, for which the former had been famous.

^d Her lover cannot leave her until the morning, when the gate shall be opened, and thus, perforce, his visit to her must become publicly known. The allusion is to the story of *Mo-sho-gun* (32), a Chinese hero, who, flying by night from his enemies, found his further progress arrested by the barrier-gate of Kan-kok'-kan, which was never opened until cock-crow. One of his followers, however, Kei-mei by name, imitated so well the crowing of a cock, that, although it was yet scarcely dawn, the gate-ward was deceived, and threw the gate wide open, so that they were enabled to pass on. The ode is from the *Jiu-i-shiu*.

^c "Yahemakura" is a species of "prunus."

c

LXIII.—Sakyo no Taifu* Michimasa.ᵃ

Now doth deep misery oppress
  My vex'd and sorrow'd mind
To none will I my woe confess,
  Save thee, among mankind:
    With thee I seek
  Of all my wretchedness to speak.ᵇ

LXIV.—Gon-chiu-nagon† Tadayori.ᶜ

By th' dim grey light of early dawn
  I stray'd by Uji's wave,
From whence the rifting mist upborne
  Me scattered glimpses gave
    Of Zeze's stakes there set,
  Whereon the fisher spreads his net.

ᵃ Son of Ishin-ko. Flourished about the time of the nengo Gen-cho (32), A.D. 1030. The ode is from the Jiu-i-shiu.

ᵇ "Would that I might tell thee myself, not by the mouth of another, how that now my thoughts are altogether intolerable to me."

ᶜ Son of Kin-to-kyo. Died in the 5th year of Cho-kiu (33), A.D. 1004. The ode is from the Sen-zai-shiu.

* "Sakyo no taifu," a rank of the 4th order in the court of the Mikado.

† "Gon-chiu-nagon," a high rank in the court of the Mikado.

LXV.—Sagami.[a]

Despised, I weep thy long neglect,
My tears drench my sleeve,
The happiness of my life is wrecked
In struggles to achieve
Thy stubborn love:
My fate might all men's pity move.[b]

LXVI.—Saki no dai-so-jo Gyoson.[c]

With thee, O mountain Sakura tree!
A lonely fate I moan,
Thy blossom only cheers me—
The only friend I own.

---

[a] Daughter of Minamoto no Yorimitz-ason, wife of Ohoi no Kin-suke.

[b] The above ode is from the *Kin-i-shiu*, where it is said to have been composed in the 6th year of *Yei-sho* (31), A.D. 1051.

[c] Died by *Nin-metz* in the 1st year of *Ho-yen* (35), A.D. 1135. The ode is from the *Kin-yo-shiu*.

LXVII.—Suwo no Naishi.[a]

Had I made of thy proffer'd arm
A pillow for my wearied head,
No longer e'en than lasts the charm
Of a spring-night's dream—what had rumour said!
    How would my fame
    Have suffer'd from men's sland'ring blame!

LXVIII.—Sanjo no In.[b]

Fain would I in this world so hard
No longer live, but still must stay:—
How wistfully my eyes regard
The midnight moonbeams' tranquil sway!

---

[a] Daughter of Taira no Tsugu-naka, Lord of Suwo, and a naishi (lady-in-waiting) at the imperial court. At an assemblage in the palace she becomes sleepy, and calls to her servant for a makura, or pillow, whereupon the Dai-na-gon Tadaye offers his arm, that she may rest her head thereon, a gallantry which the lady refuses. The ode is from the Sen-zai-shiu.

[b] Son of the Emperor Reisen. Ascended the throne in the 3rd year of K'wan-kwo (A.D. 1011); fell into distress and illness, abdicated, and died. He laments in the above ode the miserable condition to which illness and misfortune have reduced him, and envies the tranquillity of the moonlit night. He appears to have been hard pressed by the opposition of the higher Daimios, and by these forced to resign his throne.

LXIX.—No-in Hoshi.[a]

Round Mimuro-yama lustily
  The storm-winds roar and whirl,
And th' scatter'd leaves of th' momiji
  In the reddening Tatsta hurl.

LXX.—Ryozen Hoshi.[b]

In lonely solitude my home,
  And from my cabin when I stray,
Where'er my wand'ring eyes may roam,
  The landscape that doth round me lay,
    How desolate, how drear
    Doth it at autumn-e'en appear.

---

[a] Son of Tachibana no Motoyasu, Lord of Higo. The ode is from the *Jiu-i-shiu*.

[b] Nothing known of the author. The ode is from the *Jiu-i-shiu*.

LXXI.—Dai-nagon Tsune-nobu.[a]

Now twilight darkens, and the breeze
Rustles the homeside rice-fields 'mong,
And murmuring sounds my ear please,
As past my hut with thatch o'erhung
   Of Ashi grass,
The sweeping gusts of autumn pass.

LXXII.—Yuu-shi-nai Shin-wo Kenokil.[b]

Thy beauty is throughout the land
As well-known as the furious play
Of billows on Takashi's strand,
That drench the venturesome with spray,
   Who come their sweep too nigh:
So she who hath thee once beheld,
To tears of jealous love compelled,
   Her sleeve shall ne'er be dry.

---

[a] Died in the 3rd year of *Ka-ho*[c] (35), A.D. 1096. The ode is from the *Kin-yo-shiu* (36), "Collection of Golden Leaves."

[b] A *meshudo*, or concubine of Shijaku In, who flourished about A.D. 930. The ode is from the *Kin-yo-shiu*, composed at the instance of the Emperor Horikawa.

[c] According to my "Nendai-ki," there are but two years in the "nengo Ka-ho."

LXXIII.—Saki no Chiu-nagon Masaf'sa.[a]

The Sakura trees in plenty grew
On Takasago's steep hill-side,
And now their crowded blossoms show;
O may no fogs their beauty hide,
No mists from hill-top rise
To veil their radiance from our eyes.[b]

LXXIV.—Minamoto no Toshiyori no Ason.[c]

As windy blasts down Hasse's steep
In furious path impetuous sweep,
So rudely thou my suit dost slight,
And scorn thy lover's hapless plight;
No more 'ore Hasse's shrine
Will I in suing prayer incline.[d]

---

[a] Son of Oei no Chikanari. Died in the 2nd year of Ten-yei (35).

[b] The author, at an entertainment given by Oei no Ma-uchi, composes the ode as a tribute to the beauty of the Sakura trees, then in full bloom on the opposite hills. The ode is from the Jiu-i-shiu.

[c] Son of the Dai-nagon, Ts'nenobu Kyo.

[d] He had prayed at the shrine of K'wan-on (patroness of lovers) on Hasse-yama, that his mistress might lend a favourable ear to his tale of love, but vainly, for he had been repulsed with scorn. The ode is from the Sen-zai-shiu.

LXXV.—Fujiwara no Mototoshi.

A covenant thou mad'st with me,
And as the Sasame from th' dew,
So I my very life from thee
Drink in. Alas! I fear me
This autumn's days are now but few!"

LXXVI.—Ho-sho-ji no Niudo * Saki no K'wanbaku †
Daijo-daijin.[b]

In fisher's barque I onward glide
O'er th' broad expanse of ocean's tide,
And towards th' horizon when I turn
My glance I scarcely can discern
Where the white-tipped billows end,
That with the cloud-horizon blend.

---

[a] He had implored the Tenshi to grant to Kobaku (a son or other near relation) a certain dignity, and the Tenshi had promised to do so, but had put off from year to year the fulfilment thereof. Even this year again the poet fears his hopes will not be realised, as the last days of autumn are at hand, and Kobaku still waits for his elevation. The ode is from the Sen-zai-shiu.

[b] Died in the 2nd year of Cho-kwan (37), A.D. 1164, after having lived during the reigns of four Tenshi. The ode is from the Shi-ka-shiu.

* "Niudo" (入道), one who enters upon the path (of righteousness or doctrine), is a term for a priest—or the whole title means "Chief Kambaku," a priest of the order of Hosho.

† "K'wanbaku" is the title of the highest officer of the Tenshi's court.

LXXVII.—Sh'yu taku In.[a]

The brawling stream against the rock
 Its tumbling waters fiercely hurls,
Divided by the furious shock,
 In double torrent onwards whirls:
  In further flow
  I trow a single stream 'twill show.[b]

LXXVIII.—Minamoto no Kanemasa.[c]

'Tween Awaji and Suma fly
 The screaming sea-birds to and fro
Night after night; their ceaseless cry
 Doth scarce a moment's sleep allow,
  To whom his fate
  Allots the ward of Suma's gate.

---

[a] Ascended the throne in the 2nd year of *Ho-en*, and died in the 2nd year of *Cho-k'wan* (A.D. 1164).

[b] An address to the author's mistress. Tho' obstacles prevent their union at present, and cause their lives to be led in different paths, yet eventually their hopes shall be attained, and their lives be spent in common. The ode is from the *Shi-ka-shiu*.

[c] Son of Mino no Kami Kanez'ka. The ode is extracted from the *Ko-kin-shiu*, where it is said to have been composed at the instance of the Emperor.

LXXIX.—Sakyo no Tain Akisuke.[a]

When bloweth autumn's chilly blast,
   Through rifts at times the moonbeams peep,
From 'mid the dark clouds drifting past,
   And earth in pallid radiance steep,
     I love to see
   The bright-edged shadows o'er the lea.

LXXX.—Tai-ken-mon-in no Horikawa.[b]

I fear me thou wilt break the pact
   Thou mad'st with me—thy love will pass
Away from me, whom thoughts distract,
   As tangled as the unkempt mass
     My raven tresses show,
   That o'er my waking pillow flow.[c]

---

[a] Flourished about A.D. 1155. The ode is from the *Ko-kin-shiu*.

[b] Daughter of the *Dai-nagon*, Sanekyo, who flourished about the nengo *Ko-ji* (39), A.D. 1142.

[c] She is uncertain as to whether her lover will visit her again. The ode is from the *Sen-zai-shiu*, where we are told that it is one of a hundred composed at the Emperor's request.

LXXXI.—Gotokudaiji[a] Sadaijin.[e]

I heard the Hototogis[b] cry,
   I searched throughout the echoing sky,
No Hototogis could espy,
   The morning moon but met my eye.[c]

LXXXII.—Do-in Hoshi.[d]

What wretchedness is mine, O Life!
   With what deep mis'ry thou'rt oppress't!
With my sad lot I strive in strife,
   That leaveth me nor peace nor rest;
     The tears that flow
     Down o'er my cheek my anguish show.

---

[a] Entered the priesthood in the 2nd year of Ken-kiu (40), A.D. 1193. The ode is from the Sen-zai-shiu.

[b] *Hototogis* means the cuckoo bird, or some species of goatsucker. The Japanese (like the Chinese) say that it cries through the night, and does so until its eyes become bloodshot.

[c] Possibly the poet complains of the cries of the cuckoo as Anacreon of the swallow in the ode : Τί σοὶ θέλεις ποιήσω.

[d] Date unknown. The ode is from the Sen-zai-shiu.

[e] "Gotokudaiji" means 'temple of Gotoku.'

LXXXIII.—Kwo-tai-ko-gu no Taiu.^a

O'er th' world doth evil aye hold sway
I deemed, and far I fled away
    Amid the hills:
But there the deer's sad cry, too, thrills.^b

LXXXIV.—Fujiwara no Kyoske-ason.^c

Were I to linger more in life,
What seemed of old a grievous strife
Would seem to be a burden slight,
To be borne almost with delight.^d

---

[a] Became a priest in the 2nd year of An-gen (41), A.D. 1175.

[b] So that it is impossible to escape evil and its sequence misery. The ode is from the Sen-sai-shiu.

[c] Son of Sakyo no Taiu Akisuke (see Ode 69).

[d] His wretchedness takes away all wish from him to live longer. Were he still to draw out his life, his misery would become so intolerable, that he would look back upon the grief that now assailed him as a slight burden, that he would scarcely bend under.

LXXXV.—Shyunye Hoshi.[a]

With wretched thoughts distracted I
On sleepless pallet restless lay
The livelong night: with wistful eye
I waited for the breaking day
    Through chink of screen
That guards my chamber—peeping, seen.

LXXXVI.—Sai-gyo Hoshi.[b]

With deeper melancholy sways
    The moonlit night my love-sick soul;
See how my face my woe betrays,
    How down my cheek the tears roll.

---

[a] Son of Toshinori-ason. The ode is extracted from the *Sen-mi-shiu*.

[b] Son of Sai-mon no Tain Yas'kyo. The ode is from the *Sen-mi-shiu*.

LXXXVII.—J'yakuren Hoshi.[a]

The passing shower onwards sweeps,—
 Not yet upon the yew-leaves dried
Its scattered drops,—and lo! there creeps
 The rising mist up yon hill-side
  Of autumn e'en,
  At twilight's chilly hour seen.

LXXXVIII.—Kwokamon In no Betto.[b]

[The plays upon words in this Ode render it quite untranslateable, with any approach, at all events, to the force and point of the original. I have subjoined an explanation of it in the Appendix.]

LXXXIX.—Shokushinai Shinwo.[c]

Of my life or soon or late the thread,
 The withering thread perforce must snap:
I almost would 'twere now, I dread
 Of longer life the sure hap—
  The secret of our love displayed,
  For e'er our happiness low laid.

---

[a] Son of Toshinari Kyo. The ode is from the *Ko-kin-shiu*.
[b] Flourished about the commencement of the 12th century. The ode is from the *Sen-zai-shiu*.
[c] Daughter of the Tenshi Gohirakawa no In. The ode is from the *Ko-kin-shiu*.

XC.—In-fu-mon In no Taiu.[a]

I would that I might show to thee
    The island-fisher's oft-drenched sleeve,
I would that thine own eyes might see
    How the salt waves their tints ne'er thieve;
        From mine, alas!
    Aye tear-bedewed, the colours pass.

XCI.—Go-kyo-goku-ses'sho Daijo-daijin.[b]

Now grasshopper's chirp the livelong night
    I hear, now hoar-frost doth the ground
O'ercarpet, and in saddened plight,
    My day-worn raiment yet unbound,
        I strive in vain
    On lonely couch repose to gain.[c]

---

[a] Died in the 4th year of *Kem-po* (A.D. 1210). The ode is from the *Sen-zai-shiu*.

[b] Son of Goho-shoji Kanezaneko. Died in the 1st year of *Ken-yei* (42), A.D. 1206.

[c] The above is from the *Ko-kin-shiu*, one of a hundred odes composed at the instance of the Tenshi.

XCII.—Nijo no In Sanuki.[a]

My sleeve is as the rock unseen,
 Ne'er bared at lowest ebb of tide,
And none do guess my grief, I ween,
 Now how my tear-drenched sleeve's ne'er dried.

XCIII.—Kamakura no Udaijin.[b]

O that throughout an endless life
I might in peace dwell, far from strife!
For ever watch the fishing yawl,
And view the nets abundant haul:
 How fair to me,
 How pleasant such a lot would be!

---

[a] Daughter of Gohirakawa no In. Died A.D. 1165. The ode is from the Sen-zai-shiu.

[b] Son of Udaisho Yoritomo, and became Kubo A.D. 1303. The ode is extracted from the Chok'-sen-shiu (43).

XCIV.—Sangi Masatsune.[a]

Now autumn-gusts sweep
Down Miyoshino's steep,
  And far into the night so drear
The sound of beating of the cloth,
Borne to me on the night-wind forth,
  From my lonely village home, I hear.[b]

XCV.—Saki no Dai-so-jo Ji-yen.[c]

An ignorant man am I, unfit
  O'er all the multitude of men
  In dignity supreme to sit:
The simple priest's black robe again
  I would, a humble dweller on
  Wagatasoma, gladly don.[d]

---

[a] Died in *Sho-kiu* (44), A.D. 1221.

[b] In country villages the *kinuta*, or beating of newly-woven cloth to render it supple, takes place in the 9th month, towards the end of autumn. The author hearing the sound thereof, listens to it, far into the night, his memory recalling to him the hamlet where he spent his boyhood, and the old familiar customs thereof, till he fancies that he is listening to the *kinuta* of his own village. The ode is from the *Ko-kin-shiu*.

[c] Son of Hoshoji Tadamichi-ko. Died by *Niumrets*, in the 1st year of *Karoku* (45).

[d] It had been proposed that the author should become chief priest of

D

XCVI.—Niu-do Saki-no-dai-sojo Daijin.[a]

The court with Sakura's flowers is strewn
As thick as though the drifted snow
Did thereon lay: and I too soon
As withered low shall lie 'neath blow
Of man's inevitable foe.

XCVII.—Gon-chiu-nagon Sadaihe.[b]

On Mats'ho's shore, our meeting place,
At dusky hour of night, I wait
My longed-for mistress to embrace;
Ah, why then linger'st thou so late!
My ardent passion, than the fire
That heats the salt-pans, rages higher.

Hiyesan (Wagatatsoma), a position appertaining apparently to the rank of *Saki no dai-so-jo*, and the highest degree in the priestly hierarchy, which elevation he would, in his humility, excuse himself. The ode is from the *Sen-zai-shiu*.

[a] Flourished about A.D. 1227. An ode from the *Chok-sen-shiu*.

[b] Son of Toshi-nari. Entered the priesthood; died in the 2nd year of *Nin-ji* (46), A.D. 1241. He is otherwise known as Teika, and was the compiler of the present selection of odes. The above ode is from the *Chok'-sen-shiu*.

XCVIII.—Sho-san-mi Ihetaka.[a]

O'er Nara's streamlet softly blow
　　The winds in the now dim twilight,
The Misogi,[*] thereby set, show
　　That summer hath not yet gone quite.[b]

XCIX.—Gotoba no In.[c]

Some men me love, some men me hate
　　Inspire: whene'er I think upon
This miserable world, my fate
　　More pitiable doth seem to me.[d]

---

[a] Son of the *Chiu-nagon*, Mitsutaka Kyo. Died in the 3rd year of *Ka-tei* (17), A.D. 1237.

[b] The above ode is from the *Chok'-sen-shiu*, where we are told that the lines were inscribed upon a screen in the apartment of the Empress in the palace at *Nara*, the old name for the capital of Japan.

[c] Son of Takakura no In. He became Tenshi in *Ken-kiu*, was afterwards deposed by partisans of the *Kubo* or *Taikun*, and banished to the island of Oki, on the west-coast of Japan.

[d] The above ode is from the *Go-sen-shiu*, and the explanation in the *Kakchash'* suggests that it is a lament on the decadence of his power and inefficiency of his officers. His loyal servants he loves, his disloyal and tyrannical courtiers he hates, for to their evil conduct he attributes his present misery.

[*] "Misogi" are short pieces of bamboo split at the top, and having inserted in

C.—Jyuntoku In.[a]

On th' hundred-chambered palace lo[b]
A rent and tattered roof is seen,
Where rank Shinobu weeds do grow:—
How long, how hard our pain hath been![c]

---

[a] Son of Gotoba no In, whom he succeeded as Emperor. Afterwards he was deposed by Yoshitoki, and eventually he was banished to the island of Sado, about A.D. 1209.

[b] *Momo-shigi* (*vide* Appendix), *lit.* "the hundred houses, chambers, or apartments;" means also "the hundred officers of the *Dairi*," or "all the court officers." A better translation of the first line would, perhaps, be—
"On our imperial palace lo" &c. &c.

[c] The above ode is from the *Go-sen-shiu*, composed during the faction-wars of the 13th century, and a lament probably of the straits to which the Emperor was reduced by his rebellious vassals.

---

the cleft a piece of paper, on which is written a prayer or a sacred sentence. These emblems are placed in the ground always near a stream, on the last day of summer (last day of 8th moon), which in 1865 was the 14th of September.

ON JAPANESE PRONUNCIATION.

The vowels are sounded as in Italian, with few exceptions.

The consonants, single and double, as in English, for the most part, save that 'G' is always hard.

The aspirate is strongly marked.

The sound 'Hi' is peculiar, and resembles the 'hi' in the Spanish words hijo hija, anciently fijo fija.

'G,' when not at the beginning of a word, is almost equivalent to 'ng,' but is not so decided as 'ng' in 'singing.'

The 'u' in 'yu' is sounded almost like the German 'ü.'

'N' at the end of a word when the next word commences with a vowel-sound has some similarity to the Spanish 'ñ.'—

E.g.: In 'señor,' 'mañana,' &c.

'U' at the end of a word or syllable is scarcely heard, but is still sufficiently so to be distinct.

The accent in polysyllables is on the penultimate, as in the word Ihetáka, but on the ante-penultimate if the penultimate syllable end in 'u,' thus: Masátsune.

In trisyllables the accent is on the penultimate, if this is long; but if short, it is then on the first syllable.

In dissyllables the accent is on the first syllable, unless the last is long, thus: dóri. If both are long, the accent is not marked.

Generally the accentuation is not emphatic and the utterance distinct. The pitch—"timbre"—and emotional tones of the Japanese voice are different from ours, are much fuller, less shrill, and cannot be learnt except from conversing with natives, or with others who have learnt them thoroughly.

APPENDIX.

I.

Aki no ta no kari-ho[a] *no iho no toma wo arami, waga koromo-de wa tsuyu ni nuretsutsu.*

LITERAL VERSION.—"One may see through the roof of my cabin, through the thatch made of the straw of the rice-sheaves of the fields of autumn. The dew doth fall upon and wet the sleeves of my garments."

(a) "Kari-ho" is literally 'the dried sheaves.'

II.

Haru sugite natsu' ki ni kerashi, shiro tahe no koromo hos' cho ama no kagu yama.

LITERAL VERSION.—"The spring hath pass'd away, and the summer follows after it; and the secret top of Ama,[a] the drying-ground of the raiment of the white-clothed supernatural (beings) may now be seen."

(a) Ama no kagu" is the full name of the mountain which is situate in Yamato.

III.

Ashibiki[a] *no yama-dori no o no shidari*[b] *o no naga naga-shi yo wo h'tori ka mo nen.*

LITERAL VERSION.—"How can I in my loneliness sleep the night, so long, so long (as the tail of the long-trailing bird of Ashi-biki-yama, or as the tail of the long-tailed hill-fowl that trails its tail on the ground) doth it appear to me."

(a) "Ashibiki" is the name of a mountain; also it has the meaning of "long-tailed."
(b) To hang down and trail on the ground.

IV.

Tago no ura ni uchi-idete^a mireba, shiro-tahe^b no Fuji no taka ne ni yuki wa furi-tsutsu.

LITERAL VERSION.—"Just as I sally out upon the shore of Tago I look round, and lo! the snow has fallen on the high peak of Fuji (Fusi-yama).

(a) "Uchi" gives the idea of the commencement of an action. "Uchi-idete," 'just as I go out from.'
(b) White and glistening.

V.

Okuyama ni momiji fumi-wake naku Sh'ka no koye kiku toki so aki wa kanashiki.

VI.

Kasasagi no wataseru hashi ni oku shimo no shiroki wo mireba yo zo fuke ni keru.

LITERAL VERSION.—"When I see the white of the hoar-frost that lays on the bridge that gives passage to the ravens, of a truth the night is far gone."

VII.

Ama no hara furi-sake mireba Kasuga naru Mikasa no yama ni idetshi ts'ki ka mo.

VIII.

Waga iho wa Miyako no Tats'mi sh'ka wo sumu Yowouji-yama to h'to wa iu nari.

LITERAL VERSION.—"As to my dwelling in Tats'mi district nigh Miyako, 'tis so in truth, the men call the place Yowouji-yama."

(a) There is a word-play on "Yowouji," the name of a hill—"Yo-wo-uji," 'the world is evil.' Despite the ominous name, he has long dwelt there.

IX.

Hana no iro wo^a utsuri ni kerina, itadsura ni wagami yo ni furu nagame seshi ma ni.

LITERAL VERSION.—"As to love, it has faded away, alas! for

(a) "Hana no iro," lit. 'colour of flowers;' here 'love.' "yo ni furu," is explained as equivalent to "ani jo kotaeri suru."

me: the time of my loving intercourse with thee has become the time now of the long rains." She laments her lover's desertion of her.

The rendering I have in another place given of the above ode seems equally correct; but the version here given is that preferred by the *Kokin-kashi*. The former I subjoin:—

"Thy love hath passed away from me,
Left desolate, forlorn.
In winter-rains how wearily
The summer past I mourn."

LITERAL VERSION.—"Flower's tints have faded; alas! that I advance in years in this world is a circumstance which causes men to glance at me."

X.

Kore ya kono yuku mo kaheru mo wakarete wa shiru mo shiranu mo osaka no seki.[a]

(a) A word-play on "o" of "osaka no seki," o (l) 'to meet.' "Osaka" also means 'a mountain-path;' and "Osaka no seki" is the name of a place between Miyako and Ohmi' on Lake Biwa.

XI.

Wada no hara yasoshima kakete kogi ideun[a] *to hito ni wa tsugeyo Ama no tsuribune.*

(a) "Fut. deb." of *ideru*.

XII.

Amatsu[a] *kaze kumo no kayoiji fuki-tojiyo*[b] *Otome no sugata shibashi todomen.*

(a) Old genitive of "Ame," 'heaven.'
(b) Apparently 'to blow and bind,' 'to blow and stop,' the onward motion of the clouds, whereon Otome is borne.

XIII.

Tsukubane[a] *no mine yori otsuru Mina*[b] *no gawa koi zo tsumorite fuchi to nari-nuru.*

(a) A mountain in Hitachi. (b) A river in Hitachi.

XIV.

Michinoku no Shinobu-mojidzuri, tare yüye-ni midare-somen ni shi ware naranaku ni.

LITERAL VERSION.—"The *mojidzuri* of Shinobu[a] in Michinoku."

(a) "Shinobu" is the name of a place in Michinoku or Oshiu, also of a kind of plant, possibly a species of "Trichomanes." It likewise means (and herein lies a word-play), 'to suffer,' 'to endure,' 'to conceal.'

F 2

or "the Shinobu-pattern *mojidzuri*," "for the sake of (or on account of) whom am I penetrated with intricate miseries?—to my destruction."

XV.

Kimi[a] ga tame harn no no ni idete wakana tsumu waga koromo-de ni yuki wo furitsutsu.[b]

(a) "Kimi" literally 'a lord,' here 'a mistress.'
(b) Old form of "furlts" or "furishi."

XVI.

Tachi[a]-wakare Inaba no yama no mine ni oru matsu[b] to shi kikaba ima kaherflcon.[c]

LITERAL VERSION.—"Now am I about to depart. On the summit of Mount Inaba the pines are plentiful. If I hear that thou pinest for me, quickly shall I come back to thee."

(a) Observe force of "tachi," 'about to depart.' "To shi" = "to suru."
(b) This may be either "Kaheri-komu," or a future of "Kaheri-kuru"—probably the former.
(c) The word-play is on "matsu," meaning a pine-tree (8), or ' to wait for' (8).

XVII.

Chi-haya-buru[a] kami-yo mo kikadzi' Tatsta gawa karakurenai ni midz' kuguru to wa.

LITERAL VERSION.—"As to thy waters, O Tatsta! how they thread their way, ruddy-hued; even the sternly-imperious gods of old have heard not (of beauty such as thine.)" Such appears to be the meaning of this somewhat obscure stanza.

(a) Attribute of a deity. May be rendered (b) 'stern, awful,' &c., lit. (c) 'brandishing with limitless rapidity,' or (d) 'number of a thousand swords,' or again (7) 'render of a thousand rocks.'

XVIII.

Sumi-no-ye[a] no kishi ni yoru nami yoru saho ya yume no kayoi-ji h'to me yoxuran.

In the translation I have followed what appeared to me to be the best among the many explanations of this obscure stanza that I have read.

(a) Suminoye, a place in Senshiu, anciently called Sumiyoshi. The word-play is on "yoru,"—in the first instance, meaning 'to strike against,' 'fall against with an implied gentleness:' in the second, 'night,' 'dusk,' &c.

APPENDIX.   v

XIX.

*Nauihaguia on(ji)kaki aki no fashi no wa mo awode komo yo wo
sugushite yo to ya.*[a]

(a) The exact force of such phrases as "yo to ya" is difficult to render. "Ya" is an interrogative particle, "to" indicates something quoted or said,—here, something likely or proper to be said. "Yo" is merely an emphatic and sometimes vocative particle. The whole, then, may be equivalent to the French "N'est ce pas? ne le dira-t-on pas?"

XX.

Wabi-nureba[a] *ima hata*[b] *onadji Naniwa naru mi wo tukush'te mo
awan to so omo'.*

There is a word-play on Naniwa(8), a place near Miyako; *nanihoa
naru* also meaning *nan ja so i*, 'how will it end—how will things
turn out?' *Naru* also signifies 'to be in, exist at (a place).' Besides
the above, there is the following *jeu de mots* on *mi wo tukushi*:—
Mi wo tukushi (9), 'to make all possible efforts;' *mi wotsukushi* (10), a
pole set up in the water to mark the depths thereof varying with the
tide. [In the latter acceptation, the poet insinuates that his love is
so great, that his sleeve is always wet with tears, as the tide-pole with
sea-water.]

(a) Equivalent to "nangi wo sureba," 'since I am in misery.'
(b) "Ima hata" variously interpreted as "ima haiashte," 'now at last;' "ima mata," 'now again,' 'now indeed.'

XXI.

Ima kon[a] *to itishi bakari ni nagats'ki no ariake no ts'ki wo machi-
daisuru*[b] *kana.*

(a) An irregular 'future' from "kuru," 'to come.'
(b) Appears to have the force here—'to wait for the coming forth.'

XXII.

*F'ku kara ni aki no kusa ki no shikorureba Mube-yama kaze wo
arashi to iuran.*

XXIII.

Ts'ki mireba chiji[a] *ni mono koso kanashkere, wagami h'toti' no aki
ni wa aranedo.*[b]

(a) 'Various,' lit. 'thousands.'
(b) Old form of "aranuredo mo" from "aru," 'to behave,' &c.

APPENDIX.

XXIV.

Kono tabi wa nusa mo toriahedz[a] *Tamuke-yama*[b] *momiji no nishi'ki kami no ma ni ma ni.*

(a) To intend to but not actually to grasp.
(b) A mountain in Yamato (Washin),—(11), 'in front of, before me,'—thus, "Tamuke-yama" may mean 'the mountain before me.'

XXV.

Na ni shi owaba[a] *Osaka-yama*[b] *no sane-kadzura*[c] *A'to ni shirurudo kuru yoshi mo gana.*

LITERAL VERSION.—"If thou answerest to report, like unto the Sane-kadzura that grows on Osaka-yama, unknown to men, mayst thou come here to me."

(a) (12) or (13), to 'answer to one's name and reputation.'
(b) "O" (au) of "Osaka" implies 'to meet with.'
(c) "Kadzura" is also a term for the long back hair of ladies of rank. "Sane" also may be read (14).

XXVI.

Ogura[a] *-yama no momiji-ba kokoro araba ima A'to tabi no mi-yuki matanan.*[b]

LITERAL VERSION.—"The maple-leaves of Ogura, had they understanding, they would linger till the imperial train now again passed."

(a) Ogura is a hill in Yamashiro.
(b) "Matanan," equivalent to "mate' naren."

XXVII.

Mika no hara wakite nagaruru Idzumi[a] *-gawa itsu mi*[b] *ki tote ka koishi'karuran.*

(b) "Itsu mi," 'when I see,' 'shall see,' or 'have seen.'
(a) Idzumi is a river in Yamashiro.

XXVIII.

Yama-sato wa fuyū zo sabishisha masarikeru hito me mo kusa mo karenu to omohaba.

LITERAL VERSION.—"As to the hill-village in winter, its loneliness is intolerable, when I think that I shall see no man, and that all vegetation will be withered up." The word-play here is on *karenu*, which stands for *karenuru* or *kareru*, 'to dry up, wither away,'—the idiom, *hito me mo kareru*, signifying 'to see no human face.'

XXIX.

Kokoro-ate ni oraba ya oran hatsu'shimo no oki-madowaseru shiragiku no hana.

LITERAL VERSION.—"Were it my intention to pluck thee, shall I pluck thee? Will not the first hoar-frosts cheat me by resembling thee, O flower of the *Shiragiku?*"

XXX.

Ariake no tsurenaku mieshi wakare yori akatsuki bakari ukimono wa nashi.[a]

LITERAL VERSION.—"At the parting from thee, when *Ariake* is looked upon with sad envy, *Akatsuki* is indeed a wretched time."

(a) From "*aru*," 'to be,' 'become.'

XXXI.

Azusaraku ariake no ts'ki to miru made ni yoshino[a] *no sato ni fureru shirayuki.*

(a) In Yamato.

XXXII.

Yama-gawa ni kaze no kaketaru shigarami wa nagare mo ahenu[a] *momiji narikari.*

(a) "*Nagare mo ahenu,*" lit. 'not to complete the flowing on,' 'not to flow further.'

XXXIII.

Hisakata no hikari nodokeki haru no hi ni shidz'kokoro-naku[a] *hana no chiruran.*

(a) Here means 'restless, unquiet, not 'noble,' as in some dictionaries.

XXXIV.

Tare wo ka mo shiru h'to ni semu[a] *Takasago no mats' mo mukashi no tomo naranaku ni.*

(a) Old form of future dubitative of "*suru.*"

viii   APPENDIX.

XXXV.

H'to wa iza-kokoro mo shiradz furu-sato wa hana zo[a] mukashi no
ka ni nihoikeru.
    (a) Observe the force here of the emphatic particle "zo."

XXXVI.

Natsu no yo wa mada yoi nagara akenuru wo kumo no idoko[a] ni
tsuki yadoruran.
    (a) Equivalent to "idoro no tokoro."

XXXVII.

Shira-tsuyu ni kaze no fukishiku aki no no[a] wa tsuranuki tomenu
tama zo chirikeru.
    (a) More strictly, a common, or portion of uncultivated land.

XXXVIII.

Wasuraruru mi wo ba omowadz[a] chigai-teshi h'to no inochi no
oshiku mo aru kana.
    (a) Observe the construction "wasuraruru mi wo ba omowadz," equivalent to "ware wasuraruru mono de aru to omowadzite."

XXXIX.

Asaji-fu[a] no Ono no shino[b]-hara shinoburedo ama(ri)te nado ka
h'to no koish'ki.
    LITERAL VERSION.—"Though like the osier-moor of Ono (conceals) the Asajis, I would conceal (my feelings of love for thee), they are too great, and I desire so much thy love."
    (a) A name of a plant.   (b) A moor covered with a kind of small bamboo.

XL.

Shinoburedo iro ni ide ni keri waga koi wa, mono ya omo to h'to
no to made.

XLI.

Koisucho[a] waga na wa madaki tachi ni keri, h'to shiredz[b] koso
omoi-someshi ga.
    LITERAL VERSION.—"As to the fact of my love (for thee), the fame thereof has quickly become public; yet how anxious was I that men should not know of it."
    (a) Explained in the "Kokubash'" as equivalent to "Koi wo suru to i(fu."
    (b) Passive negative of "shiru" (15), 'to know,'—may be translated here as a negative potential.

XLII.

Chigiriki-na katami-ni[a] *sode wo shiboritsutsu*[b] *Suye no matsu-yama nami kosaji to wa.*

(a) Equal to "Tagai ni," 'reciprocally.'
(b) "Sode wo shiboru," lit. ' to wring one's sleeve, to weep abundantly.'

XLIII.

Ai-mite no nochi no kokoro ni kuraburaba, mukashi wa mono wo[a] *omowazari keru.*

LITERAL VERSION.—"When I search my heart after having been with you (I find) that of old (before I knew you) I was not sad."

(a) "Mono wo omo," 'to be sad.'

XLIV.

Ai kite no tabetashi nakuba[a] *naka naka ni h'to wo mo mi wo mo uramizaramaji.*

(a) "Tabetashi nakuba" means 'were to cease and be no more.'

XLV.

Aware to mo if[a] *beki h'to wa omohoede, mi no itadu'ra ni narinu-beki kana.*

LITERAL VERSION.—"Thou might'st have had pity on me, but thou passest me with indifference: of how great misery to me art thou the cause."

(a) "Aware wo if" 'to have pity on.'

XLVI.

Yura[a] *no to wo wataru funa-bito kaji wo tahe yuku-ye wo shiranu, koi no michi kana.*

(a) Name of a place in Kii; also of another in Tango.

XLVII.

Yahemugura shigereru yado no sabishisha ni h'to koso mihene, aki wa ki ni keri.

The probable meaning is that given in the translation.

APPENDIX.

XLVIII.

Kaze wo itami iwa utsu nami no onore no mi kudakete, mono wo omo koro kana.*

LITERAL VERSION.—"The waves, driven by the wind, strike the rock (they are dashed into spray); my happiness (affected by your disdain of my love, is broken up. I am now very sad, at heart."

(a) To suffer from the wind.

XLIX.

Mi-kaki-mori Yeji no taku hi wo yoru wa moyete, hiru wa kiketsutsu, mono wo^a kao omoku.

(a) "Mono wo omo" (18), 'to be sad.'

L.

Kimi ga tame oshikarazarishi inochi saha nagaku mo gana to omoikeru kana.

LITERAL VERSION.—"On account of thee, O my mistress! I cared for life; how heartily I wish it may last ever so long."

LI.

Nageki-tsutsu h'tori nuru yo no akuru ma wo ikani hisash'ki mono to hazcashiru.^a

(a) Equivalent to "Obonshimeshi wo aru."

LII.

Wa'roji no yuku-suye made wa katakurebe ka wo kagiri no inochi to mo gana.

LIII.

Kaku to da ni^a yoya^b wa Ibuki no sashi-mogusa mo shiraji na^c moyuru omoi wo.

(a) 'As to the condition in which I am now.'
(b) "Yoya Ibuki, ya iwanu (difficile dictu)." Ibuki is also the name of a hill in Omi.
(c) "Shiraji" is negative of "shiru," 'to know,' and also has the significance of 'white, unspotted.'

LIV.

Akeureba kururu mono to wa shiri-nagara nawo uramishi ashorako kana!

APPENDIX.   xl

LV.

Takino oto wa takute kikashite nariwatado, na kozo nagarete nawo kikahakeri.

LVI.

Arazuwa kono yo no hoka no omoi-de ni ima h'to tabi af' koto mo gana.

LITERAL VERSION.—"The thought arises in me of going to a world other than this, which shall soon be not. O that I might once more now meet thee."

LVII.

Meguri-aite mishi ya sore to mo wakanu ma ni kumo-gakure ni shi yo-ha no ts'ki kana.

LVIII.

Arima-yama Ina no sasawara kaze fukeba ide-so-yo⁸ h'to wo warere ya wasuru.

   (a) (17) 'One who matches with, is comparable to.'

LIX.

Yasurawade⁸ nenamaji mono wo sayo fukete katabuku made no ts'ki wo mishi kana!

   (a) "Yasurawade," 'to wait and be disappointed.'

XL.

Ohoye-yama Ikuno no michi no tohakereba mado 'umi mo mish' Amenohashidate.

The following plays on words are herein met with :—
Ikuno,¹ ² the name of a place in Tango.
 ,, ³ 'the road by which one goes to—"
 ,, ⁴ equivalent (according to the *Kakehashi*) to *ikura no hiroi ni*, 'over so many broad plains,' or 'over so broad a plain.'
Fumi,⁵ a footstep, to walk, to tread upon.
 ,, ⁶ handwriting, especially of a woman.
With these explanations, the various possible translations of the stanza will be easily effected.

¹生 ²野 ³行之道 ⁴幾 ⁵跡 ⁶書狀

LXI.

Inishihe no Nara no Miako no yahezakura kyo Kokonohe[a] *ni nihoi-nuru kana.*

(a) Anciently written "Kokono-he," but now "Koko-no-he," 'the place or locality here.' Hence a play upon words.

LXII.

Yo wo komete tori no sora ne wa hakaru tomo yo ni Ausaka no seki[a] *wa yurusaji.*

Yo ni ou is explained as equivalent to *yo ni fuwa* (*vide* Append. Ode ix.), and with this signification—the latter clause of the verse would insinuate that the lover, however dexterous in the art of evading difficulties, could never overcome the obstacles that prevent his satisfying his love for the authoress.

(a) Ausaka no seki is a place in Omi.

LXIII.

Ima wa tada omoi taenan to bakari wo h'to-dzute[a] *narade if*[b] *yoshi mo gana.*

(a) Message or communication by a third person.
(b) "If" is pronounced "iu," like 'you.'

LXIV.

Asaborake Uji[a] *no kawa-kiri tae-dake ni arawaro-wataru Sez*[b] *no ajiroki.*

LITERAL VERSION.—"'Tis dawn. Here and there, in the rifts of the mist that hangs over the river of Uji, come into my sight the net-stakes of Seza."

(a) Uji, a river in Omi, falling into Lake Biwa. (b) Seza is on Lake Biwa.

LXV.

Urami-wabi hosanu sode da ni aru mono wo koi ni kuchinan; na kozo oshikere.

LXVI.

Morotomo ni aware to omoke yama zakura hana yori hoka ni shiru h'to mo nashi.

LXVII.

Haru no yo no yume bakari naru ta-makura ni kahi-naku[a] taka na kozo mikere.

(a) "Kahi-naku," (1) 'inelegant, improper, &c.'

LXVIII.

Kokoro ni mo arade uki yo ni nagarahela koishikarubeki yo-ha no ts'ki kana.

LXIX.

Arashi fuku Mimuro no yama[a] no momiji-ha wa Tatsa no ogawa no nishki narikeri.

(a) Mimuro-yama is in Yamato.

LXX.

Sabishi sa ni yado wo tachi-idete nagamureba idoko mo onaji aki no yaugura.

LXXI.

Yuumereba kadota no inaba otodsureto ashi no maroya[a] ni akikaze wo fuku.

(a) Lit. 'circular house,' here 'a thatched hut.' "Kadota" is the term given to a rice-field situate close to the house.

LXXII.

Oto ni kiku[a] Takashi[b] no hama no adanami wa kakeji ya sode no nure wo koso sure.

The word-play is on *adanami*:—

Adanami,[1] 'a roller or vast wave breaking on the shore,' or 'tide at the turn.'

,, 1 & 4 'a vain inconstant man,'(19) equal to 'womanish, weak, &c.,' 'changeable.'

(a) "Oto ni kiku" is a phrase meaning 'renowned, celebrated, famous.'
(b) Takashi is in the province of Idsumi.

¹化 ²浪 ³各 ⁴身

APPENDIX.

LXXIII.
Takasago[a] *no onohe no sakura sakini keri to-yama no kasumi tatadi mo aranan.*[b]

(a) A hill in Harima.   (b) "Aranan," probably equivalent to "aru nara na."

LXXIV.
Ukarikeru h'to wo Hatsu[a] *no yama oroshi hageshikare to wa inoranu mono wo.*

(a) A hill in Yamato.

LXXV.
Chigiri okishi Sasemo[a] *ga tsuyu wo tnochi nite aware gotoshio n aki no tsumori.*

The meaning of this stanza is somewhat obscure. *Inumori* is explained as equivalent to *inu-yos'*, *inu* being negative of 'i,'[1] 'to be in;) yos',[2] 'appearance, fashion, mode of being, &c.'

(a) "Sasemo-gusa."(20)

LXXVI.
Wada no hara kogi idete mireba hisakata no kumoi ni mago oki[a] *tsu shiru-nami.*

(a) "Oki," 'the deep-sea, blue water.'   "Tsu" is the old genitive termination.

LXXVII.
Se wo hayami iwa ni sakururu taki-gawa no warete mo suye ni awan to zo omo.

LXXVIII.
Awaji[a] *shima kayo chidori no naku koye ni iku yo nezamenu Suma*[b] *no Seki-mori.*

(a) Awaji, a large island not far from Ohosaka.   (b) Suma, in Setsshiu.

LXXIX.
Aki-kaze ni tanabiku kumo no taka-ma yori more iduru ts'ki no kage no sayakesa.

LITERAL VERSION.—"From the opening rifts in the clouds,

¹居   ²様子

which the autumn winds have spread thinly over the sky, glints out the beauty of the moonlight and its shadows." Note the force of *more-idreru*, *moru* being used primarily to signify the action of water soaking through and dripping from anything.

LXXX.

Nagakaran kokoro mo shiradz kuro kami no midareta kesa wa mono wo koso omohe.

LXXXI.

Hototogisu nakitsuru kata wo nagamureba, tada ariake no ts'ki zo nokoreru.

LXXXII.

Omoi-wabi' satemo inochi wa aru mono wo uki ni takeru wa namida narikeri.

LXXXIII.

Yo no naka yo michi koso nakere omoi iru yama no oku ni mo sh'ka zo naku naru.

LITERAL VERSION.—"In the world there is neglect of righteousness (there is but evil). Even among the wilds of the hills, wherein I have thought to penetrate, the deer's cry resounds."

LXXXIV.

Nagaraheba mata konogoro ya shinobaren ushi to mishi yo zo ima wa koishiki.

LITERAL VERSION.—"As I continue to live on, even now do I endure much suffering. What seemed an evil world to me is now regretted by me" (*i.e.* the longer he lives the greater becomes his misery).

LXXXV.

Yo mo sugara[a] mono omo koro wa akeyarade neya no hima sahe tsurenakari-keru.

LITERAL VERSION.—"Towards the end of night, when I was

(a) (E) The ending of the night.

harassed with sad thoughts, the dawn had not yet broken ; even as to the chinks in my sleep chamber I was wretched (because they transmitted no signs of the welcome day-break).

LXXXVI.

Kageki[a] *tots ti'ki-ya wa mono wo omoeuraru kukuji kao naru waga namida kana.*

(a) To sob, lament, &c.

LXXXVII.

Murs-same[a] *ao tsuyū mo made hinu*[b] *maki no ha ni kiri tachinoboru aki no yūugure.*

(a) A shower, a passing shower.   (b) Not to be dry.

LXXXVIII.

Naniwa-ye no ashi no kari-ne no h'to yo yuye ni wo takushi yo koi-wataru-beki.[a]

The word-play here is on *Kari ne no hioyo.*—1st, (22) 'One joint of a reaped stalk (of Ashi).' 2nd,¹ 'A passing visit of one night only,' with the (1st) rendering, the sense of the whole will be :—"I have been with you for a space (of time), as short as the space of a joint of a reaped stalk of *ashi* that grows by Naniwa's creek, and &c." With the 2nd :—"I have enjoyed but a passing embrace with you for one night only (a time as short as the stubble of the *ashi* of Naniwa's creek, and I will exert my utmost that our love may endure."

(a) To go on loving.

LXXXIX.

Tama no o[a] *yo tayaba takekuss nagarahcbs shinoburu*[b] *koto no yowari wo so suru.*

(a) (23) Lit. 'the thread of a jewel,' a thread by which a jewel is suspended, here 'the course of life' metaphorically.

(b) To mood in secret, as lovers do, ' to conceal, hide.'

借寢之一夜

XC.

Mixboyama Ojimu no ama no sode da ni mo murc ni zo nurrahi iro wa kawards.

(a) "Iro" means 'colour, hue,' also 'love, passion, &c.' "Misrla yma" is equivalent to "misetai," the optative form of "miyuru," 'to cause to see, to show.'

XCI.

Kirigtris' naku yu shimo yo no samushiro ni koromo-kataahki* h'tori ka mo nen.

LITERAL VERSION.—"The grasshopers are chirruping. This night, on the carpet of hoar-frost (or in the cold of the hoar-frost), sleeping with my head on my arm, how can I, if alone, gain repose?"

(a) "Samushiro" is the name of a kind of mat. "Samushi" means 'cold,' also 'desolate, solitary.'

(b) "Koromo-kataahki" appears to signify the act of supporting one's-self on one elbow or arm, and thus sleeping without taking off one's dress.

XCII.

Wagu sode wa shiho-hi ni miheau oki no ishi no h'to koso shiraru kawaku ma mo nashi.

LITERAL VERSION.—"As to my sleeve, 'tis as the rock in deep water, not seen at low tide. Men know it not; and there is no dry spot thereon."

XCIII.

Yo no naka wa tsune ni mo gamona nagisa kogu ama no kobune no tsuna-de wo kanashi.

LITERAL VERSION.—"How desirable is the life here on earth. How pleasant to watch the net-haul of the small boats of the fishermen plying near the shore."

XCIV.

Miyakino no yama no aki-kaze sayo fukete furu sato arazaku koromo utsu nari.

(a) Far into the night.

XCV.

Ohoki-naku uki-yo no tami ni ohokuran Wagaiatsuma ni sumi-zome no sode.

LITERAL VERSION.—"Must I, though unfit, preside over the

people of the empire. (No! may I don), the black-dyed sleeve on Mt. Wagatasoma."

XCVI.

Hana sae/ arashi no niwa no yuki narade furi-yuku mono wa wagami nari-keri.

LITERAL VERSION.—"It is not snow *(yuki)* on the courtyard, but blossoms strewn there by the blast. As to the falling of snow (i.e. by word-play—as to the advancing in years) I am such." There is a word-play here on *furi-yuku*, which (*yuku* being almost identical in sound with *yuki*, 'snow') may mean "the falling of the snow," or "the advancing in years."

XCVII.

Konu h'to wo Mats'ho no ura no yuunagi[a] ni yaku ya mo shiko no mi wo kogaretsutsu.

There is here a word-play on *Mats'ho; mats'* signifying 'to wait for, expect.' Mats'ho is in the island of Awaji. *Yaku ya mo shiko* is explained as equivalent to (34), q.v. *Ya* probably means 'place or hut,' and thus the literal version would be :—"In the pleasant evening, on the shores of Mats'ho, I wait for you, who come not. I become as the burnt-up and parched sea-weed and salt in the furnace-house (where the brine is boiled down to make salt)."

(a) The exact meaning of "yuunagi" (25) q.v. is doubtful.

XCVIII.

Kasu myogu Nara no o-gawa no yuugure wa misogi zo natz' no shirushi nari-keru.

XCIX.

H'to mo oshi h'to wo urameshi ajiki-naku[a] yo omof' yuwe ye ni mono omof' mi wa.

(a) Equivalent to (26) or to (27) q.v.

C.

Momo-shigi-ya furuki nokiba no shinobu ni mo nawo amari aru mukashi nari-keri.

LITERAL VERSION.—"As to the *shinobu* on the decayed roof of the hundred-chambered palace, ah! too plentiful is it, and this since many years." There is a word-play on *shinobu*, which means 'a kind of weed,'[22] and also 'to suffer, endure.'[23]

INDEX.

EXPLANATION OF ABBREVIATIONS.

Pr. n. 'proper name,' pl. 'place,' mt. 'mountain,' isl. 'island,' riv. 'river,' impl. 'temple,' v. 'vide,' v. a. 'verb active,' v. n. 'verb neuter,' lit. 'literally,' dub. 'dubitative,' caus. 'causative,' neg. 'negative,' p. 'page,' incl. 'inclusive,' cond. 'conditional,' par. 'particle,' part. 'participle–ial,' met. 'metonomy,' Roman characters refer to the Odes, Arabic characters refer to the pages.

A.

Abe no nakamaro, pr. n. vii.
Adanami, vide Append., Ode lxxii.
Agatamori, pr. n. vii. (a)
Aimiru, to see, to meet and see, to see mutually
Ajikinaku, v. Append., Ode xcix.
Ajiro, a kind of stake-net made of slender bamboos
Akadoki, dawn of day
Aka some yemon, pr. n. e. lix.
Akenuru, equivalent to akeru, akuru
Akeyarade, neg. participial form of ake-yaru, 'to become daylight'
Aki, autumn
Akisuke, pr. n. e. lxxix.
Akuru (akeru), to open, to grow light, to dawn
Ama, a fisherman, also (1) 'heaven'
Amagawa,1 'Milky-way,' lit. 'heaven river'
Amanohashidate, pl. v. lx (c)
Ama no kagu, a mt. e. App. ii.
Angen, nengo, A.D. 1175—1176 incl.

Anwa, nengo, A.D. 908—969 incl.
Arami, to see through, to see daylight through (as the holes in a tattered roof &c.), explained in the Kakshash as having a force equivalent to saku sumi mi
Aranedo, for aramaredomo cond. neg. form of aru
Arashi, a storm, gale
Araware (ru), to become evident
Ariake,2 term for a moon that shines all night
Arima, pl. v. Append. lviii.
Ariwara no Narihira, pr. n. v. xvii.
Aru, to be, to have
Asaborake, dawn, the early morn.
Asajiu, pl. xxxix. (b), Saccharum spicatum [Thunberg Fl. Jap.], also called tsubana
Asalada, pr. n. e. xliv.
Ashi, pl., Phalaris arundinacea [Thunberg Fl. Jap.]
Ashibiki, name of a mountain, also 'to saunter, to drag the feet after'

'天川   '有明

INDEX

Ason, v. "Cat. of Titles"
Ate'tada, pr. n. v. xliii.
Au, to meet; by met, to love
Ausaka, a path up a mountain, name of a place
Awade, neg. part. form of au
Awaji, isl. v. Append. lxxviii.
Awamu—all } fut. dub. form
Awan—au   }
Aware, compassion, pity—wo i u, 'to have compassion on; also 'alas! wretched!'
Awo, pr. n. v. xvii. (a)
Azuchi fuji maro, pr. n. xviii. (b)

B.

Ba, the same as ha
Bakari, only, just
Beki,¹ equivalent to Latin bilis, only met with as a terminal form of verbs
Betto, v. "Cat. of Titles"
Biha, banjo, v. x. (b)
Biobu, a screen
Bitats, pr. n. v. xxxvi. (b)
Bummu, name of an emperor, v. xxvii. (a)
Bun toku,² pr. n. (a)
Bun toku jits' rok', v. "Catal. Jap. Works".
Bunya no Asayasu, pr. n. xxxvii.
Bunya no Yasuhide, pr. n. xxii.

C.

Chidori, a kind of sea-bird
Chigiriki, preterit form of chigiru,³ 'to make a vow or promise'
Chi haya buru, v. Append. xvii.
Chiji ni, variously, v. Append. xvii.
Chikuzen, a province of Nippon

Chiu na gon, v. "Cat. of Titles".
Chiru, to scatter, disperse, blow away as the wind does the leaves
Chō (toi), place or position where verb's action occurs, or material object (not agent) by means of which verb's action is affected
Cho kiu, nengo, A.D. 1040—1043 incl., v. Table of Char.
Chok' sen shin, v. "Cat. Jap. Works"
Cho'k'wan, nengo, A.D. 1163—1164 incl., v. Table of Char.

D.

Da, subject or matter of discourse, condition, fact, &c.
Daigo, pr. n. v. xxxvii. (b)
Dai ho, nengo, A.D. 701—703 incl.
Dai jō dai jin, v. "Cat. Titles"
Daikaku, temple in Saga
Dai na gon, v. "Cat. of Titles"
Dai ni, v. "Cat. of Titles"
Dai toku ono, v. ix. (a)
De, for sode, a particle, which as a post-position 'by means of'
Dō in, pr. n. v. lxxxii.

F.

F'ke ni keru, old form of past tense of f'keru, 'to grow late'
Fuchi, deep water
Fuji, name of Fusiyama
Fujiwara, a place used at one time as a capital city
Fujiwara no Okikaze, pr. n. vide xxxiv.
Fujiwara no Toshiyaki, pr. n. v. xviii.
Fujiwara no Tsunaisana, pr. n. xv. (a)

¹可 ²文德 ³契

Fujiwarano Yoshitaka, pr. n. l.
Fukishku, to blow with a continuous sweep
Fuki tojiru, to blow-stop, to cease blowing, to lull
Fuku, to blow
Fumi, to tread on, to walk on
Fumi-wake, to tread underfoot and make way through
Funabito, a sailor, boatman, fisherman
Funamori, pr. n. v. vii. (a)
Furau (furu)
Furimake-miru, to contemplate or look round at, with the head lain back and the face upturned
Furi-yuki, to advance in years, to go on getting old
Furu, to grow older [yo ni furu as a location may mean 'to love mutually as men and women;' senjo no kataraí sûru is a Jap. explanation]
Furu,² to fall down, to pour, as rain, snow, &c.
Furuki, old, ancient
Fushi, an internode or joint of a bamboo, &c.
Fusiyama (Fujisan), a celebrated volcano, about 40 miles from Yokohama—height 12,000 feet. Always called Fuji san by the natives
Fuyu, winter

G.

Ga, an adversative particle, almost equivalent to 'but;' an emphatic use; a genitive post-particle
Gamona,² desirable, pleasant

Gana, the same as kana, an emphatic word at the end of a phrase often denoting wonder and expressing a desire
Gen-ji monogatari, v. "Cat. Jap. Works"
Genkei, nengo, A.D. 876—885, v. Table of Char.
Gi-do-san-shi, pr. n. v. lii.
Genaho, nengo, A.D. 715—716 incl. a. iv. (a)—a Table of Char.
Gon-chin-nagon, v. "Cat. Titles"
Gohirakawa, an emperor's name
Gohoshoji Kanesaneko, pr. n. v. p. 47 (b)
Go-kyo-goku-sessho, pr. n. or title, v. xci.
Go-sek'ku, v. xii. (b)
Go-san-shiu, v. "Cat. Jap. Wka."
Gotoba no In, posthumous name of an emperor, v. xcix.
Gotokudai, name of a temple
Kotoshi (Gotoshi). It is like (that which precedes), it is thus, accordingly, so, similar
Gyôson, pr. n. v. lxvi.

H.

Ha,² a leaf
Hageshki, violent, rude, stormy
Hama, beach, strand, shore
Hana, flower [Hana no iro, a phrase signifying 'enjoyment of love']
Hara, lit. 'plain' [ama no hara, 'vault of heaven']
Haru, spring
Haru-mia, pr. n. v. xvii. (a)
Haramichi no Tsuraki, pr. n. xxxii.
Hashi (hash¹), a bridge
Hasse, mt. v. Append. lxxi.
Has-shimo, the first or earliest hoar-frost

Mayamu, to quicken
Hei jo, pr. n. v. xvi. (d)
Hi,¹ sun, day, light
Higashi san jo sumiho Kane ihe, pr. n. v. 28 (a)
Hikari, light, brilliance, splendour
Hima, crevice
Hime miko, a title, princess, royal highness
Hinu, negative form of héru,² 'to dry, become dry
Hiru, daylight, day as opposed to night
Hisash'ku, for a long time
Hisakata, the heavens, the skies
H'to, man (homo)
H'to maro, v. "Cat. of Titles"
H'tori, alone, by one's-self
H'toshiu, the same as A'tomaro
H'tots', one
Hiuen, province of Japan
Ho, rice-sheaf or bundle
Ho an, nengo, A.D. 1120—1123 incl. v. Table of Char.
Hoka (no),³ outer, other
Hon Jiu, pr. n. v. xliii. (a)
Horikawa, an emperor, v. 38 (b)
Hos', v. a. to dry, to put out to dry
Hoshi, v. "Cat. of Titles"
Hosho ji, tmpl.
Hototogis', swallow, or some kind of goatsucker
Hoyen, nengo, A.D. 1135—1140 incl., v. Table of Char.

I.

Ibuki, pl. v. Append. liii.
Ideshi, past tense (book language form) of idzuru, 'to go out, sally forth, &c.'
Idemoyo, v. Append. lviii.

Idete (idzuru)
Ida'ko,⁴ ids're no tokoro, 'where! in what place!'
Idzmi shkibu, pr. n. v. lvi.
Idzumi, a province of Nippon
Idzmi, riv. v. Append. xxvii.
Idzuru, to go, go out, sally forth
Ihetaka, pr. n. v. xcviii.
Iho, old form of ihe, 'house, hut, &c.'
Itashi—tu, preterit form
Ika ni, how! how much! howsoever!
Iku,⁵ how much! how many?
Ikuno, pl. v. ix. (a)
Ima, now, at once
Ima hata, v. Ode xx.
In, v. "Cat. of Titles," often signifies 'a college or monastery or brotherhood,' as in Tai kun mon in no Horikawa [Horikawa of the brotherhood of Tai kun mon]
Ina, pl. v. Append. lviii.
Inaba, a district in Nippon, v. xvi.
Inaba, the rice-plants, the rice-plants and their long leaves, the foliage of rice-plants
In fu mon in, pr. n. v. xc.
Inishiye, old, ancient, most anct.
Inochi, life
Inoru, to pray to, adore, implore
Inumari, v. Append. lxxv.
Iro, colour, tint, lust, desire
Iru, to be in, to enter, penetrate
Ise, name of a princess, v. xix.
Ise no Ohosuke, pr. n. v. lxi.
Ishi, a stone, a rock
Ish'kawa maro, pr. n. v. ii. (a)
Ishin, pr. n. v. 31 (a)
Ishiyama, pl. v. 6 (a)

¹日 ²幹 ³外 ⁴何 ⁵所 ⁶幾

Itadsura, 'mischief;' *ai quel dommage, c'est dommage*
Itamu, *lit.* to hurt, spoil; *kaze ni itami*, as used here, means, 'by the violence of the wind'
Its', a princess, v. xvii. (a)
Iu, to say, speak, call, name
Iuran, the same as Iu
Iwa, rock, stone
Iza kokoro, a mental condition of doubt, uncertainty

J.

Ji n go i no ge, v. 'Cat. of Titles'
Ji go i no ge Kanehobu, pr. n. v. 26 (b)
Jin i shin, v. "Cat. Jap. Works"
Ji to, name of an emperor, v. ii.
Ji yen, pr. n. v. xcv.
Jyakuren, pr. n. lxxxvii.
Jyuntoku In, posthumous name of an emperor. c.

K.

Ka, interrogative particle
Ka,¹ fragrance
Kadota, *lit.* door-rice-field, a rice-field close to the door or hut
Kage, shadow, or abstractedly the contrast between light and shade
Kagiri, end, limit, boundary, termination
Kagu, to be secret, hidden, &c.
Kahuru, to return
Kaheri kon, either *kakeri koms*, or *kakeri kuru*³
Ka hi naku, v. Append. lxvii.
Kaho, *nengo*, A.D. 1094—1096 in. v. Table of Char.
Kaho, face, visage
Kaji, a rudder

Kakeji ya, v. Append. lxxii.
Kaki no moto, pr. n. v. lii. & notes
Kakoji, radical form of *Kakats*, 'to lament, be inwardly sad'
Kaku to da ni, in this condition, thus, in such a condition as my present one
Kamakura, pl. in Sagami
Kami, god, hair of the head
Kami yo, age of the gods
L'ampei, *nengo*, A.D. 859—897 incl., v. Table of Char.
Kana, an emphatic particle at the end of phrases
Kanashi [in Ode 93] explained in *Kokubash* as equivalent to *omoshiroi*,³ 'pleasant, delicious, &c.'
Kanashki, also *kanashi*, sad, pitible, wretched, what induces sadness or misery
Kaneuka, pr. n. v. xxvii.
Kan ke, v. xxiv.
Kan kok'kan, pl. v. lxii.
Kara, after
Karakurenai, reddish, ruddy, brown-hued
Karenu, probably for *karenuru*, old form of *karuru*, 'to wither, become dried up' (*h'to mo mo kusa mo kareru*, not to see a human form, and to be in a place where the vegetation has all dried up — as it does in winter)
Kari, reaped, cut
Karine, v. Append lxxxviii.
Karoku, *nengo*, A.D. 1225—1226 incl., v. Table of Char.
Kasasagi, raven
Kasuga, name of a district in Jap.
Kas'mi, fog, mist

Kata, place, quarter, position
Katabuku, to incline downwards, to set (of the moon)
Kataku, hard, difficult
Katami ni, mutually, on each side; also sometimes,—in memory of
Kataahki, to sleep with the head on one's arm
Katei, nengo, A.D. 1235—1237 incl., v. Table of Char.
Kawa, river, often gawa
Kawaku, to dry, be drying, or dry
Kawara, pr. n. v. xiv.
Kawara in, impl. v. xlvii. (e)
Kawaru, to change
Kawashiru, exact sense of this word [which is in none of my native dictionaries] not apparent
Kayo, to pass on
Kayoiji, path, of anything passing on, or passing to and fro
Kaze, wind
Kei mei, pr. n. v. 33 (d)
Kem po, nengo, A.D. 1213—1219 incl., v. Table of Char.
Ken giu,¹ 'dragging-ox;' name of a constellation comprising part of Aquarius and Capricorn
Ken toku, pr. n. v. xlv.
Ken yei, nengo, A.D. 1206, v. Tab. of Char.
Keri, an old preterit termination
Kesa, this morning
Keu² (kyo), to-day
Ki, tree — radicle of kuru, 'to come'—preterit form as in chi-giriki
Kibi daijin, pr. n. v. vii. (a)
Kiharu,⁵ to go out, become extinguished
Kikoharu (Kita), a passive form

Kiku, to listen, hear
Kimi, lord—poetically, 'mistress'
Ki ni karaahl, have ceased to come
Kinota, v. p. 49 (b)
Kinotomonori, pr. n. v. xxxiii.
Kino Tsurayuki, pr. n. v. xxxv.
Kin seki monogatari, v. "Cat. Jap. Works"
Kin Lau, pr. n. v. lv.
Kin to, pr. n. v. 34 (b)
Kin yo shiu, v. "Cat. Jap. Wks."
Kiri, mist
Kioto, the ordinary term of the Miyako or capital
Kirigiris, grasshopper
Kisaki, queen or spouse
Ki sen, pr. n. v. viii.
Kishi, coast, shore
Ko, v. "Cat. of Titles"
Kobaku, pr. n. v. 40 (a)
Kobune, boat, small vessel
Kogarura, to become burnt or charred
Kogi, a scull
Kogi idsuru, to go forth by rowing
Kogan, pr. n. an emperor, v. xxxviii. (c)
Koi, love
Koi'cho, the fact of being in love
Koi-wataru, to seek to gain the love of some one
Koji, nengo, A.D. 1142—1143 in. v. Cat. of Char.
Ko kin shiu, v. "Cat. Jap. Wks."
Kokonohe, v. Append. izi.
Kokoro, heart, sense, intelligence
Kokoro-ate, intent in a, purpose
Komu—kuru, fut. dub. 'to come'
Kono, 'this,' used with a noun fol.
Kore, 'this,' used generally without a noun following

Koremada, pr. n. v. xxiii. (a)
Koro, time, epoch, instant
Koromo, an old word—'garment,' more accurately 'outer garment'
Koromo de, sleeve
Kosaji (kos') negative radical form from kos', 'to cross, get across, pass over, &c.'
Kosh kibu, pr. n. v. ix.
Ko sho, pr. n. u. iii. (c)
Koso, rather, certainly, indeed—frequently used as an elegant redundancy
Koto, matter, affair, fact—after a verb gives this an infinitival, sometimes a substantival force
Koye, voice, cry
Kubo, v. "Cat. of Titles"
Kuchi nan = kuchi naran, from kuchiru or kuts'ru, 'to crumble into decay'
Kudaku, to break to pieces, shatter into atoms
Kuge, v. "Cat. of Titles"
Kuguru, applied to the flowing of water among obstacles, and partial ralentissement thereof
Kumo, cloud
Kumo gakure, cloud-darkening
Kumoi, cloud-wall, the firmament, the empyrean
Kurabu, to compare with
Kuro kami, black hair
Kuru, to come, arrive
Kururu, to darken, become evening
Kusa, grass, herbs, as distinguished from ki, 'shrubs or trees'
Kwanbaku, v. "Cat. of Titles"
Kwan kwo, nengo, A.D. 1003, v. Table of Char.
Kwo ko, v. xv.

Kwo ka mon In, pr. n. lxxxviii.
Ken kiu, nengo, A.D. 1190—1198 incl., v. Table of Char.
Kwo tai ko gu, v. "Cat. of Titles"
Kyoake, pr. n. v. lxxxiv.
Kyowara no Fukayaba, pr. n. v. xxxvi.
Kyowara no Mats'to, xxxvi. (b)
Kyowara no Moto'aka, pr. n. xlii.

M.

Ma, interval, spot, place, portion of time, place, or circumstance
Mada, yet, still
Made ni, up to, until
Machidetzuru, to go out and wait for, or to wait for the sallying forth of
Madaki, quickly, without delay
Mago, apparently means in lxxvi. 'to become blended with'
Maki, a kind of yew-tree
Man yo shin, v. "Cat. Jap. Wks."
Maro ya, round hut, a sort of rude dwelling, with thatched roof, often used by hermits
Masafsa, pr. n. v. lxxiii.
Masari (ru), to be in excess
Matanan = machi naran, a fut. dub. of matz', 'to wait for'
Matsu,[1] a pine tree; (b) to wait for, hope for, expect
Me, eye, sight
Meguri au, to go out and look for some one
Mei kake, a concubine
Mi,[2] myself, ours'-self, self; (4) radical of miru, 'to see, behold, look at'
Miako, capital city, Kioto
Mibu no Tadami, pr. n. v. xli.

¹松 ²待 ³身 ⁴見

Mibu no Tadamine, pr. n. v. xxx.
Michikane, v. 29 (b).
Michimasa, pr. n. v. lxiii.
Michinari, pr. n. v. xxxiv. (c).
Michinobu, pr. n. v. liv.
Michinoku, name of a province, Oshiu.
Michi no omi, a pl.
Michi taka, pr. n. v. 28 (b).
Michi tsuna, pr. n. v. li.
Midare(ru), to be in confusion, physical or mental
Midare some, to be penetrated with confusion, trouble, &c.
Mide', ? water (?) not to see
Mijikaki, short, brief (of space and time)
Mika (Mikawa), a province of Nippon
Mikado, v. "Cat. of Titles"
Mikaki mori, v. "Cat. of Titles"
Mikasa, name of a mountain
Miki, an old preterit form from miru
Mikoto, v. "Cat. of Titles"
Mimuro, mt. v. Append. lxix.
Mina, name of a stream
Minamoto no kanemasa, pr. n. lxxviii.
Minamoto Minoyuki, pr. n., v. xxvii.
Minamoto no Shigeyuki, pr. n. v. xlviii.
Minamoto no Yorimita, pr. n. v. 85 (a)
Mine, summit, peak
Miru, to see, look at, behold
Misogi, v. note xcviii.
Mi wo takuahi, v. Append. xx.
Miyoshino = Yoshino
Miyuki, v. xxvi. (d)

Mo, also, and—intensitive or emphatic particle
Mojidsuri, v. 9 (d)
Mogusa = moxa, a common Artemisium used as local cautery
Momiji, generic name of maples
Momoshigi, v. c.
Mono, thing, person, he, she, or it, who, which, &c.
More idsuru, to drip out of, shine out of
Morotomo ni, together, in company—no, 'all of them'
Mosho gun, pr. n. v. 33 (d)
Motoyasu, pr. n. v. 28 (a)
Motoyoshi, pr. n. v. xx.
Moyuru, to be consuming, burning away
Moxa (mogusa)
Mube, mt. v. Append. xxii.
Mukashi, old, ancient, long ago—(if repeated) 'once upon a time'
Murasaki shikibu, pr. n. v. lvii.
Murasame, a sudden shower of rain

N.

Na, name, fame, reputation—an adjectival termination, a contraction for namaru
Nadoka, 4 how ! how much ! ever so greatly, &c.
Nagaku (-ki -shi), long
Nagame, for naga ame, long rain, continuous rain
Nagamuru, to glance at, take a look at
Naga nagashi, poetic for nagashi, 'which see'
Nagara, lit. 'interval;' may be translated after a verb by 'whilst, although, &c.

¹陸奥 ²水 ³不見 ⁴奈何

INDEX.

Nagare mo ahenu, not to continue to flow on
Nagarura, to be flowing on
Nagatsuki, 'long moon,'—that is, the 9th month
Nageku, to bemoan, bewail
Nagisa, beach-shore—or perhaps the water near the shore
Naho, more, rather
Naishi, v. "Cat. of Titles"
Naka naka ni, for naka ni, 'profoundly, extremely, to the core, &c.
Naka nota'kasa no ta-in, v. "Cat. of Titles"
Nakuru, do not, is not
Nakitsuru, an old form of naku
Naku, to cry, scream, &c.—said of animals
Nami, wave
Namida, a tear
Nani, what? how?
Na ni shi ou, v. Append. xxv.
Nani wagata, pl. v. Append. xix.
Nara, pl. v. Append. lxi.
Naru naku = naranu or naku-naru
Nari, the simple copula,—is, — as
Nariakira, pr. n. v. 31 (c)
Naru, to become, to be, to be in, as Kasuga naru yama, 'the hill in Kasuga'
Naruhashi, v. "Cat. Jap. Works"
Nashi, is not—also (from naru) becomes, causes to be, &c. — causative form of naru
Natsu, summer
Nen, fut. dub. of neru, 'which are'
Nemamaji, the same as ne naru maji, will not sleep, cannot sleep

Neya, sleeping-chamber
Nezamenu, negative form of nezameru, lit. 'to sleep,—awake,' involves the idea of a continuous natural sleep throughout the night
Ni, a post-position, 'in, with, by,'
Nihoi, to smell at, perceive odour of
Nihongi, the same as Nippon ki, v. "Cat. of Jap. Works"
Nijo, a pl. near Kioto
Nijo no jo In Samaki, pr. n. v. xcii.
Ninji, nengo, A.D. 1240—1242 in. v. Table of Char.
Ninjin, nengo, A.D. 851—853 in. v. Table of Char.
Nin wa, nengo, A.D. 885—888 incl. v. Table of Char.
Nin wo,1 human king, the name given to the latter dynasty of Mikados
Nish ki, v. xxiv. (c)
Niudo, v. "Cat. of Titles"
Niumei, pr. n. v. xv. (a)
Niumetsu,2 to enter destruction, v. xii. (a)
Niwa, a court-yard
No, genitive post-particle,—a common or portion of unlaboured land
Noboru, to ascend
Nobutaka, pr. n. v. 31 (a)
Nochi, after, with no preceding; succeeding, with no following
Nodokeki, for nodoka, 'pleasant temperature'
No in, pr. n. v. lxix.
Nokiba, eaves of a roof
Nokoraru, passive form of nokoru, 'to except, take out of'

人王　入滅

INDEX

Nururu, to be wet [midz' ni nururu, to be wet with water]
Nuretsuten, old form of past tense of nururu
Nuru, used for nern, 'to get to sleep'
Nusa, v. xxiv. (b)

O.

O, tail
Ogawa, small river, brook
Ogura, mt. v. Append. xxvi.
Oho, to preside over, preside over as protector
Ohoi, riv. v. 15°
Ohoi no Chikanari, pr.n. v. 59 (a)
Ohoi no Kius'ka, pr. n. v. 35 (a)
Oho kei da', v. "Cat. Jap. Wks."
Ohoke naku,¹ unfit, unequal to
Ohanakatomi, v. "Cat. of Titles"
Ohosaka, a city about 80 miles from the capital Kioto
Ohoshi ka-uchi no Mitsune, pr. n. v. xxix.
Ohoye, pl. v. ix. (c)
Ohoye no Chisato, pr. n. v. xxiii.
Ohoye no Masatoki, pr.n. v. 29 (c)
Ojima, small islands, islets, name of several places and of some isle-clusters
Oki, isl. v. xl. (c)
Okimadowasern, to put on and cause to deceive, to be on and cause to deceive
Oku (okishi), to put, place, set, sometimes to do, perform
Oku, interior, inland [okuyama, inner, and therefore wilder, hills]
Omi, one of the provinces of Nippon
Omo,² to think, to believe, to regret

Omohoyede,³ (omohoheds), not to perceive, not to take notice of
Omoi waharu,¹, ⁴ to ask of, implore
Onaji, the same, alike
Ono, pl. v. Append. xxxix.
Onohe, (80) peak of a hill
Ono no Komachi, pr. n. v. ix.
Onora, reflective pronoun, 'one's-self, his-her-itself'
Ono teijin. v. ix. (a)
Oroshi—in yama oroshi, 'a hill-gust of wind'
Oru, to break, break off
Oru,⁵ to grow (tokoro ni, 'to be growing in any place')
Osaka no seki, pl. v. Append. x.
Osaka yama, mt. v. Append. xxv.
Oshi, loveable, praiseworthy, excellent
Osh'karu, to be loveable, regrettable,—sometimes 'lamentable'
Oshiu, a province in N. E. of Nippon, otherwise Michinoku—q.v.
Oto, noise [nikriko, 'famous, renowned']
Otodzureto, rustling, making a sound
Otome, name of a (6) or goddess
Otomonoła', v. vi. (a)
Oto no kiku, v. Oto
Ots', pl. in Omi
Otsuru, to fall from a height downwards

R.

Reisen, pr. n. of an emperor. v. 25 (b).
Ryo sen, pr. n. v. lxx.

S.

Saugi Takamura, v. xi.

San jo, an emperor, v. lxviii.
Sasabara, a plain covered with a kind of small bamboo
Sasemo (plant)
Sashi (sasu), to press down upon, to apply something to
Sashi mogusa, a species of moxa plant (*Artemisium*)
Saso. The only *saso* I can find in Jap. dict. means 'to lead on, allure on.' In xcvi., *Hana saso arashi* probably means 'the wind that allures the flowers' from the plum-trees
Satemo, alas! alas!
Sato, village
Sayakesa, equivalent to *sayakesa* 'purity, brightness, splendour'
Sayo fukuru,[1] to become late (said of the night)
Se, course, or flowing, or current of a river
Sei, pr. n. v. lxii.
Sei rei aik'ki, v. "Cat. Jap. Wks."
Sei shi rok', v. "Cat. Jap. Wks."
Sakaruru, to become arrested or stopped by some obstacle
Seki, a barrier-gate
Seki mori, guard of a *seki*
Semi maro, pr. n. v. x.
Sen (fut. dub.) *suru*
Sen sai shiu, v. "Catal. of Jap. Works"
So wo hayami, to hasten onwards the current
Sabishiki, lonely, solitary
Sabishisa, loneliness, solitude
Sachin sho, v. "Cat of Titles"
Sadaihe, pr. n. v. xcvii.
Sa dai jin, v. "Cat. of Titles"
Sadakata, pr. n. v. xliv. (*b*)

Sagami, pr. n. v. lxv. ; also name of a province in Nippon
Saga no Yamada, a pl. v. ii. (*a*)
Saho,[3] a poetic word, equivalent sometimes to *made, tomo*, &c.
Sahe mon no taiu Yaskyo, pr. n. v. 45 (*b*)
Saigyo, pr. n. v. lxxxvi.
Saka no uye no Korenori, pr. n. v. xxxi.
Saki ni keru, past form of *saku*, 'to burst into bloom'
Saki no chiu nagon, v. "Cat. of Titles"
Saki no dai so jo, v. "Cat. Titles"
Sakura, a kind of tree (*prunus sp.*)
Sakyo no taiu, v. "Cat. of Titles"
Sammi, pr. n. v. lviii.
Samashiro, a kind of mat on which one sleeps
San dai jitsu roku, v. "Cat. of Jap. Works"
Sanokadara, plant, xxv. (*b*)
Sane kata, pr. n. v. liii.
Sangi Hitoshi, pr. n. v. xxxix.
Sangi Masatsuna, pr. n. v. xciv.
Shi, radical of *suru*
Shibashi, for an instant, briefly
Shiboru, to wring (out the water)
Shide kokoro naku, (probably) trembling, unquiet
Shigarami, dyke or weir across a river — here 'a mass of dead leaves acting more or less as a dyke'
Shigayama, pl.
Shigururu, to be grown over thickly
Shiho, sea-water, tide, salt
Shiho hi, low-tide
Shihoruru, soaked, wet through, to wet, or be wet through

[1] 更深　[2] 副

INDEX.

Shigaku, an emperor, v. 38 (b)
Shi k'wa shiu, v. "Cat. of Jap. Works"
Shima, an island
Shimo, hoar-frost
Shin ko kin shiu, v. "Cat. of Jap. Works"
Shinoba, to conceal, hide, fear, suffer, endure—name of a plant—name of a hill in Oshiu
Shin wo, v. "Cat. of Titles"
Shiragiku, pl. (a kind of chrysanthemum), v. xxix. (a)
Shiraji, negative radical of *shiru*, or 'white, lustrous, unspotted, pure'
Shiranami, white wave
Shirareru, to be known, to get to know
Shira tsuyū, white dew
Shira yuki, white or brilliant snow
Shiroki, white, pure, whiteness
Shiro tahe, dazzling-white
Shiru, to know, to be acquainted with
Shirushi, to make known, a sign of
Sh'ka, deer
Sh'ka so, thus it is, yet—a poetic form of *sh'karu zo*
Shogun, v. "Cat. of Titles"
Sho hei, *nengo*, A.D. 931, v. Table of Char.
Shoichi, v. Cat. of Titles"
Shokujo,¹ lit. 'weaving-woman'—the name of the star *Wega*, a, in *Lyra*
Shokushinai, pr. n. v. lxxxix.
Shonagon, v. "Cat. of Titles"
Shorokuinojo, v. "Cat. Titles"
Shyunye, pr. n. xlxxxv.
Shyutoku, pr. n. v. lxxvii.

Sode, sleeve
So jo, v. "Cat. of Titles"
Some (ru), to dye
Sone no Yoshitada, pr. n. v. xlvi.
So sei, pr. n. a. xxl.
Sora, that (not generally used with a noun)
Soyogu, to blow softly—*soyosoyo f'ku*
Sugara, † end, termination
Sugata, form, appearance, shape, semblance, person
Sugu, to pass on, pass by, pass over
Sugusu, to overpass, transgress, come to the end of, terminate
Suma, pl. v. Append. lxxviii.
Suminoye, pl. v. Append. xviii.
Sumi zome, black-dyed
Sumu, to live on, dwell on
Suwo, pr. n., v. lxvii,—also a province of Nippon
Suye, mt. in Oshiu
Suye ni, up to the end of

T.

Ta, rice-field
Tabi, time, epoch (*konotabi*, 'this present time')
Tachibana naramero, pr. n. v. viii. (c)
Tachi wakaru, to rise and depart
Tada, only, just, but
Tadaye, pr. n. v. 36 (a)
Tada yori, pr. n. lxiv.
Tago, pl. v. Append. iv.
Taha dahe ni, by openings here and there
Tahoma, a spot where there is deficiency of
Tahoru, to be deficient, to become exhausted, to put an end to, stop

¹織女   ¹終

INDEX. xliii

Tai-ken-mon-in no Horikawa, pr. n. v. lxxx.
Taikun, s. "Cat. of Titles"
Taira no Kanemori, pr. n. s. xl.
Taira no Tsugu naka, pr. n. v. 35 (a)
Tais, s. "Cat. of Titles"
Taki hashi nari jun, pr. n. v. 33 (a)
Takakura, pr. n. v. 51 (c)
Takane, lofty peak or summit
Takasago, pl. v. Append. xxxiv.
Takashihama, pl. s. Append. lxxii.
Take no Uchimakune, pr. n. v. xxxiii. (a)
Takera, pr. n. s. vi. (a)
Taki, waterfall
Taki gawa, cascade-like stream
Taku, to set on fire
Tama, jewel, ball, drop
Ta makura, arm-pillow, the arm on which one rests the head as on a pillow
Tame ni, for, on account of, for sake of
Tametoki, pr. n. v. 31 (a)
Tamba, a province of Nippon
Tami, people, populace
Tamuke, mt. v. Append. xxiv.
Tanabiku, to spread thinly over, to lie in thin masses over
Tanetsugu, pr. n. s. vi. (a)
Tango, a province of Nippon
Tare, 'who?
Tachi (tats), to arise—tatan
Tate mi, v. vili.
Tatsta, name of a stream
Tei ka, pr. n. v. 50 (b)
Tei shin, pr. n. s. xxvi
Ten ji, pr. n. v. l.
Ten kei, nengo, A.D. 938—946 incl. s. Table of Char.

Ten mu, pr. n. s. ii. (a)
Ten ryak', nengo, A.D. 947—956 incl. v. Table of Char.
Ten shi, v. "Cat. of Titles"
Ten toku, nengo, A.D. 957—960 in s. Table of Char.
Ten yen, nengo, A.D. 937—937 in s. Table of Char.
To, a particle indicating that what precedes is quoted, or implying that—also a copulative particle
Todomuru, to remain, stop, linger, stay at rest
Tohoku, to be distant
Toki, time, period, when
Toki mochi, pr. n. v. 32 (a)
Toki yas', pr. n. v. xv. (a)
Toma, thatch, roof
To mai, v. Ode i, note (a)
Tomenu, not to stop
To mo, to particle, and mo particle, equivalent to 'as well as'
Tomonoyoshino, pr. n. s. vi. (a)
Toneri, pr. n. xxxvi.
Tori, to take, a bird
Tori abeds, v. Append. xxiv.
Toshi, to particle, and shi radical of suru, 'to do, act'
Toshimoto, v. pr. n.
To te, represented by a Japanese character apparently equivalent to to sh'te, or to omōte
Tou, to ask, demand
Toyama,¹ other hill
Toshi nori, pr. n. v. 45 (a)
Tsu, old genitive post-particle
Tsubana = osajia, a kind of plant
Tsukubane, name of a mountain
Tsugu (guru), to tell, inform
Tsuki, moon, month
Tsuku',² to exhaust

¹ 外山　²尽

Tsumori, to accumulate, grow bigger, deeper, fuller
Tsumu, to pluck, pull
Tsuna-de, the rope of the net by which it is hauled in
Tsune ni, always, continually
Tsune nobu, pr. n. v. lxxi.
Tsune nori, pr. n. v. 29 (b)
Tsuranuku, to penetrate among, perforate
Tsuromaku, expressive of a countenance full of grief, angry and sad
Tsuribune, angling-boat, fisher-boat
Tsutan, an old preterit form
Tsuyu, dew

U.

Uchi idsuru, to go out, sally forth; uchi denotes commencement of an act; uchi idete, 'just as one goes out,' 'as soon as one goes out'
Uda, pr. n. v. x. (b)
Udaijin, v. "Cat. of Titles"
Uji, pl. v. Append. lxiv.
Ukarikeru, to be unsteady, inconstant
Uki'ushi, evil, miserable
Uki yo, 'floating world,' universe, empire
Ukon, pr. n. v. xxxviii.
Un ki, nengo, A.D. 715—716 incl., v. Table of Char.
Ura, bank or margin (of a lake, &c.)
Urameshi'ki, hateful
Uramu, to dislike
Utsuri, to fade, wither,—as said of life, beauty, &c.

W.

Wa, post particle, indicating— sometimes a nominative case; sometimes a separation of a phrase from the rest of the sentence
Wabinuru = wabiru, exact meaning not apparent, explained as equivalent to *wa gi wo suru*, probably signifies 'to implore of, ask of'
Wada no hara = unahara,[1] the open ocean
Waga, 'I, mine,' sometimes 'he, his'
Wagami, myself
Wagaiatsuma, mt. v. Append. xcv.
Wakana, 'young vegetable,' *Brassica orientalis*
Wakanu, to group, encircle; in Ode lvii. probably has the sense of 'recognize'
Wakareru, to be separated, to be parted from
Wakaru, to divide, separate, part from—v. a.
Waku, to boil—v. n.
Ware, the personal pronoun 'I'
Warete (waru), to divide into parts
Was'reru, to be forgotten, abandoned
Was'ru, to forget, abandon
Wataru,[2] lit. 'to cross over, to take passage to,' more especially 'by water,'—here probably (3) 'to seek for,' (*koi wataru*) 'to seek after love'
Watasuru, to cause to cross over, to give passage to

[1] 和田原 [2] 渡 [3] 亘

INDEX

Wo, post particle, generally denominating accusative case

Y.

Ya, an expletive particle, an interrogative particle, — also (1) night; and (2) a house, dwelling (in comp. chiefly)
Yado, a house, hut, dwelling
Yadoruru, to find place in, to rest in
Yahomugara, pl. xlvii.
Yahozakura, sp. of *Prunus*
Yakamochi, pr. n. v. 6
Yaku, to burn—v. a.
Yama, mountain, hill
Yamabe no Akah'to, pr. n. v. lv.
Yamadori, hill-fowl (a sort of pheasant) ?
Yamagawa, hill-stream
Yamashina, a pl. in Yamato
Yamato, a province of Nippon
Yamato monogatari, a "Cat. of Jap. Works"
Yamazakura, wild *sakura*, a species of *Prunus*
Yamasato, hill-village
Yasoshima, 'eighty isles' on the west-coast of Nippon
Yasumasa, pr. n. v. 29 (c)
Yasuran, to wait and meet (a person), to wait for
Yasyuhe, pr. n. v. xli. (a)
Yei dai nen dai ki, a "Cat. of Jap. Works"
Yei so, *nengo*, A.D. 980
Yaji, v. "Cat. of Titles"
Yekeo, pr. n. v. xlvii.
Yen ki, *nengo*, A.D. 901—922 incl. v. Table of Char.
Yen shiu, province of Nippon, otherwise Tohotomi

Yeya Ibuki=ye Iwazu, v. Ap. liii.
Yo,¹ night; an appellative particle; (2) world, life, existence; age, generation (a)
Yogura, to put aside, remove
Yo ha,¹,⁵ midnight
Yo hi,⁷ night-time
Yo mo sugara,⁶ end-night — towards the end of night
Yori, from, than
Yori moto, pr. n. v. 27 (a)
Yoritomo, pr. n. v. 48 (b)
Yoru, to be against, fall against or upon; (2) night, evening
Yosei, pr. n. v. xiii.
Yo shi, good, excellent, ' It is well '
Yoshino, pl. v. Append. xxxi.
Yoshinobu, pr. n. v. xlix.
Yowari, end, termination
Yowonji, name of a hill near Kioto
Yuki, snow; also root-form of *yuk-u* 'to go, proceed '
Yuki hira, pr. n. v. xvi.
Yuku, to go, proceed
Yuku ye, *lit.* going and coming, path
Yume, a dream
Yuru uo to, pl. v. Append. xcvi.
Yuugure, evening, dusk
Yuunagi, exact meaning not apparent—*lit.* evening calm
Yuu ahi nai shin wo Kenokii, pr. n. v. lxxii.
Yuuzuru, to grow dusk, become evening
Yuyu, because of, amount of, *propter*

Z.

Zaza (or Saza), pl. v. Append. lxiv.
Zo, an emphatic particle

夜 家 世 代 半 行 宵 終

ADDENDA AND ERRATA.

Mojidzuri (Ode xiv.) is also the name of a curiously-marked rock on Mt. Shinobu, in Oshiu.

For an explanation of *Yomouji* (Ode viii, line 3) the reader is referred to the Appendix.

IN TRANSLATIONS,

Page 4, Ode 6, line 2—for *where* read *when*.
,, 4, note (a), ,, 4— ,, *shiu* ,, *mi*.
,, 5, ,, (a), ,, 2— ,, Anki ,, Uski.
,, 10, ,, (a) . . . ,, *tachi ware* ,, *tachi wakare*.

IN APPENDIX,

Ode 17, line 2—for *yoraran* read *yoguru*.
,, 17 ,, 7— ,, *sirfuo* ,, *simite*.
,, 20 ,, 6— ,, toWushi ,, ta'Tushi.
,, 21 ,, 3— ,, karu ,, kuru.
,, 21 ,, 4— ,, force here ,, force here of.
,, 27 ,, 1— ,, nayararu ,, *nagururu*.
,, 28 ,, 5— ,, karemo ,, karemu.
,, 31 ,, 2— ,, shirayaki ,, shirayuki.
,, 33 ,, 1— ,, kohoro ,, kokoro.
,, 34 ,, 1— ,, ha ,, ka.
,, 61 ,, 3— ,, oow ,, *nowo*.
,, 65 ,, 1— ,, nazarabeba ,, nagarnheba.
,, 75 ,, 1— ,, gotoshio n ,, gotoshi no.
,, 86 ,, 1— ,, Kageki ,, Nayeki.
,, 89 ,, 1— ,, ianaba ,, tuhenaba.

IN INDEX,

Article *Ji go i no ge Kane* line 1—for Jo go i no ge Kaneshobu read Jiu go i no ge Kanenobu.
,, *Arami* line 5—for aska read *aku*.
,, *Aranado* ,, 2— ,, ara ,, *aru*.
,, *Ashi* ,, 1— ,, arundinacea ,, arundinacea.
,, *Naruheshi* ,, 1— ,, naroheshi ,, narubeshi.
,, *Ninjiu* ,, 1— ,, ninjiu ,, ninjiu,
,, *Omoiwabaru* ,, 1— ,, wabaru ,, wabiru.
,, *Uto* ,, 1— ,, nikiko ,, — ni kiku.
,, *Sawo* ,, 4— ,, asashi ,, arashi,
,, *Yuyo* ,, 1— ,, amount ,, on account.

CATALOGUE OF TITLES

OF THE AUTHORS OF THE PRECEDING ODES.

---o---

Ason 朝臣 *lit.* 'Court official,' a vassal, attendant on the Imperial court at Miako, a dignity of the 3rd or 4th class.

Botto 別當 an official rank, of which the duties and position are unknown to me.

Dai jin 大臣 'high officer,' title of a person having an official position at the Court of the *Dairi*; a dignity of the 2nd and 5th classes.

    Sa dai jin 左大臣 left-hand or superior ⎫
    Nai dai jin 内 ｜ ｜ Inner or middle ⎬ degrees of the rank *Daijin*.
    U dai jin 右 ｜ ｜ right-hand or inferior ⎭

Dai jo dai jin 大政大｜ 'high officer and Illustrious administrator,' the title of the highest office in the *Dairi's* court—a dignity of the first class.

Dai ni 大贰 *lit.* 'Great Second,' a rank attributed to the Lady Sammi in Ode 58.

Dai sho 大將 'Great Leader,' a dignity of the fourth order.

    U dai sho 右大將 right-hand or inferior ⎱ degree of the rank
    Sa dai sho 左 ｜ ｜ left-hand or superior ⎰ *Dai-sho*.

Gon Chiu Na gon a subdivision of the rank *Chiu-nagon*, v. *Nagon*.

CATALOGUE OF TITLES.

Ho shi 法師 — *lit.* 'officer of rites or customs,' properly a term for a priest of Buddha.

H'tomaro equivalent to *Ason.—q.v.*

In 院 'Court, College &c.,' a posthumous imperial title.

Ju go i no ge 從五位下 Lower division of the second class of the fifty order of rank. *Sho go i* 正五位 would mean the first class of the *Go i* 五位 or fifth order.

Ko 公 equivalent, perhaps, to our 'duke,' or to 'nobleman.'

Kuge 公家 a courtier in the *Dairi's* court.

Kubo 公方 imperial personage, or princely; a common title of *Taikun*.

K'wanbaku 關白 title of the highest officer but one in the court of the *Dairi*; a dignity of the first class.

Kwo tai ko gu 皇太皇后 *Kwo ko o* means 'the imperial empress;' and the former seems to be the name of an officer in attendance on her.

Mikado 御門 royal corner or gate; a designation of the *Tenshi*.

Mikoto 尊 honourable or pre-eminent.

Mikakimori 御垣守 'Captain of the Guard of the Imperial Palisades.'

Nagon 納言 high officers in the court of the *Dairi*.

Dai nagon	大	Superior Officer of	3rd order
Chiu nagon	中	Middle " "	
Sho na gon	小	Inferior " "	4th

CATALOGUE OF TITLES.

Naishi 内侍 — 'those who wait within,' a term for the emperor's 12 wives, or sometimes for a lady-in-waiting.

Niudo 入道 — a term for a bonze—see notes to Ode 76.

Oho naka tomi 大中臣 — vide notes to Ode 49.

Sa chiu sho 左中将 — a rank next to Daisho.

Saki no 前 — chief or first.

Shinwo 親王 — heir-apparent or sometimes prince of blood royal.

Sho ichi 正一位 — first division of the first order of rank.

Sho roku i no jo 正六位上 — upper division of the first class of sixth order of rank.

Sho gun 将軍 — 'a leader in war,' a designation of the temporal emperor.

So jo 僧正 — 'Buddhistic rectitude' a rank among the priests of the monasteries of Mt. Hiye.

Dai so jo 大僧正 — the superior or chief So jo.

Tai kun 大君 — the temporal emperor, a term, 'great prince,' never used by the natives.

Ta iu 大夫 — 'eminent one,' a rank of 5th and sometimes 6th class.

Sa kyo no ta iu 左京大夫

Naka tsukasa no ta iu 中敢大夫

Ten shi 天子 — 'heaven-son,' Emperor, or *Mikado*, or *Dairi*.

Ten wo 天王 — 'heaven-king,' Emperor, or *Mikado*, or *Dairi*.

Where "Fujiwara" occurs in a name, it must be taken as the name of a place where at one time the Court was held. "No" gives a genitive force to the word preceding it.

CATALOGUE OF JAPANESE WORKS.
REFERRED TO IN THE PRECEDING PAGES.

Chok'sen shiu 勅撰集
Collection of Selections made at the command of the Emperor.

Genji monogatari 源氏物語
History of Affairs of the Original Families.

Go sen shiu 後撰集
Collection of After-selections.

Hon cho bun sui 本朝文粋
Which probably means "Official purity in Japan."

Jiu I shiu 拾遺集
Collection of Additional Pieces.

Kin seki monogatari 今昔物語
Relation of Events Ancient and Modern.

Kin yo shiu 金薬集
Collection of Golden Leaves, a miscellany of short poems.

Ko kin shiu 古今
Collection of Odes Ancient and Modern.

Man yo shiu 萬葉
Collection of 10,000 Leaves.

Mei getsu ki 明月記
Records of Illustrious Months.

CATALOGUE OF JAPANESE WORKS.

Nippon ki 日本記
Records or Description of Japan.

Narubeshi 南留別志
A Treatise on Errors of Words and Misapplications of Phrases.

Oho kei da' 大系圖
Complete Panorama of Families.

Sei rei nik'ki 蜻蛉日記
Daily Jottings in the Land having the similitude of a Dragon-fly (i.e. in Japan)

Sei shi roku hon 姓氏綠本
Book of the Catalogue of Family Names.

San dai jits roku 三代實錄
True Catalogue of the Three Dynasties.

Sen sai shiu 千載 |
Collection of pieces written during a period of 1,000 years—or probably, Collections of a Thousand Records.

Shi ka shiu 詞花 |
Poetical Anthology.

Shin ko kin shiu 新古今 |
New edition of the *Ko-kin-shiu*.

Yei dai nen dai ki 永代年代記
An Epitome of Japanese History.

Yamato mono gatari 大和物語
Relation of the Affairs of Yamato.

TABLE OF NENGO CHARACTERS.

An 安	Chi 治	Ho 保	Ji 兒	Ka 字	Ko 護	Ro 老	Tai 大
Chi 安	Chiu 雄	Ji 八	Jiu 壽	Kai 衡	Ko 衡	Roku 祿	Tai 泰
Cho 治	Do 中	Ka 長	Kei 嘉	Kan 化	Kwa 化	Sei 錄	Tei 貞
Do 銅	Fku 長	Kei 景	Ken 同	Kwan 觀	Kwan 寬	Shi 至	Ten 天
Gen 元	Hak 白	Ken 建	Ki 銅	Kyo 亨	Man 萬	Shin 神	Toku 德
Hei 福	Ho 平	Ki 乾	Kiu 龜	Mei 明	Mon* 文	Sho 勝	U 島
Ho 保		Kiu 久	Ki 喜	Nin 仁	Rei 靈	Sho 承	Un 雲
		Kits 吉		Reki 曆	So 祚	Sho 昌	Wa 和
						Sho 正	Wo 應
						Shu 朱	Yei 廷
							Yen 養
							Yu 弘

* or Bun.

TABLE OF CHARACTERS.

IN TEXT.

2 大夫 · 天川 12 東風菜 17 幸行
16 錦 27 文武 32 孟嘗兒 33 入道

IN APPENDIX.

1 迨 2 松 3 待 4 千甲振
1 千劍破 6 千磐破 8 何者成
9 身盡 10 儒標 11 手向 12 名頁
13 歷各 14 眞寐 15 知 16 物思
17 是富人 18 無甲斐 19 妒娜人
20 芭天哉 21 終夜 22 刈根之一節
22bis 玉之緒 24 燒藻壇 25 夕和
26 味氣無 27 詮無 28 垣衣 29 思

百人一首

英國京都倫敦印刷

丙寅年十一月 申雅客筆

�95 前大僧正慈鎮 わがそのくうに己乃ひ子わ旦守の
　けふこのきぞ於うき暮なれ此柚�96 入道前大政大臣 花さそ
ふ嵐乃には庭ぞふりゆく物ハあらずもわがみなりけり
�97 権中納言定家 来ぬ人をまつほの浦にタかぎにせ
くえしほのもしほたれつ々㊞ 従二位家隆 風そよぐ
ならの小川のタぐれハみそぎぞ夏のしるし成ける
㊞後鳥羽院 人もをしく人もうらめしあぢき
なく世をおもふゆゑに物おもふ身ハ
㊞順徳院 百しきや古き軒端のしのぶにもなほあまりある昔なりけり

⑩ 殷富門院大輔 見せばやをしまの海士
の袖だにも濡れぞ濡れし色はかはらず ㉛ 波高き松枝改
大政大臣 きみぐ吹鳴也それ松乃さむしろにこ諸
ものとしき楊々ねん ㉜ 一條院撰枝承袖八志ほひ
ふ見へぬ伊乃石乃今をそ吾ねのわくほもれし
乃を礼の一穗でのふしも ㉝ 倉右大臣 きれ中八次千もごもあ渚こぐ伝凌
㉞ 後々條雅經みらし
乃白鳥秋風さよふれて過るさとにをくれ聲ふり

㊅優婆塞咋ちもすぐやうも死わもみしろ八ゆやぞ

祢せのひ半千へれむ系りけり㊆霊坊法咋ぞぞ

きとて夕やハゝ死をむちハ次るもちの自むる

我房の郎㊆寂運法咋むらさめ北而も陶ごひ

凶祢孔義ふにきわ去死㊆る枕孔夕ぐれ

㊆皇嘉漾〇商誰皮之死芦死の行祢比一狡仲

魚みをつくしてや㊆式子内親巳玉乃

緒与稔尔八拿へ収尓㌍八弱ふるるのうちりそ

一 ゑぞらんやも志く史黒髪乱みぐれてさ八今の
をてゑ思第 ⑧ 後徳大寺左大臣 本とぎ次鳴る
のこをゑすむれバ島で有明乃月ぞおれ伙
⑧ 足因法師 おもひ旦びさてもふ命八わ原物を
うきにふ生へぬ八寄をごや年れり ⑧ 皇太后宮大夫俊秉
与此中を逆ると志けおもひ際山乃奥にも志
うぞ鳴る方湯 ⑧ 藤原清情朝臣 ゑぞのふへバ南し此
此せ志礼をれんうしとみ甚ぞ今八煮しき

煞り並しさせもが荻を今日て、あれとゝしの秋も
いぬ先に㊆法性寺入道前関白太政大臣 心あの原
ちこ出て見れバ久堅の雲のをち海のふをきろっと波
㊆崇徳院 瀬をせみ岩ぞせをるを澎川れつれて
も末にわハんとぞ思ふ㊆源兼昌 あえぢ崎の通ふ
千鳥れふくこに爰狼祢ざめぬ須磨のせきや
㊆左京大夫顕輔 秋風い空をたびく雲の耗る
らいそれ出る月の影のさやけさ㊆待賢門院堀川

を立出てあをのむれバいづこもおもじ秋の夕ぐれ
⑦大納言経信 夕されバ門田の稲葉おとづれて芦の
まろ屋に秋風ぞ吹く ⑦祐子内親王家紀伊
音にきく高師の浜のあだ浪はかけじや袖のぬれ
もこそすれ ⑦前中納言匡房 高砂のをのへの桜
さきにけりとやまのかすみたゝずもあらなん
⑦源俊頼朝臣 うかりける人をはつせの山おろし
らえだしかれと八祈らぬものを ⑦藤原基俊

㊻ おぼろけにみるびりさぬ袖ぞふあく袖を恋ふく
ちるこん忍了そ惜れれ ㊿ 能大僧正けうる僧ともふ
わ八れと思へ山ざらの桜ちれけさのふもほる人もなし
㊻ 周防内侍 春此夜此夢バのけれはを枕ふのひ
ゑくなんれ忍了そ惜れれ ㊽ 三條院 心ふもゆぞうれ
ゑそうへバこひしかるべきねばまのつきの形
㊾ 能因法師 嵐ぬくみ実の出此紅よば人もちるの川
れにしきちりけたり ⑦ 良暹法師 さびしさにやど

さらく濱での月を見しより ⑥⓪ 小弐新内侍 大江山戴笠
のそ）のをぬれれ袖さぞぬみもみぢ天のもしき
⑥① 伊勢大輔 いにしへのならの都の八重桜
ふる里に。ほひぬばこの歌 ⑥② 清少納言 夜をこめ
て鳥のそら祢ハはかるともよに逢坂の関ハゆる
さじ ⑥③ 左京大夫道雅 今ハただ思ひ絶れんと八
かりを人つてならでふよしもがな ⑥④ 権中納言定家
がり顔ほうけそなほやも家こぐ小舟ハれ春る儘じ野兒ま

ORIGINAL TEXT.

㊺ 恋しきとはたれつけそめし名ならむをしりてみだるゝ我が心かな

㊻ 大納言公任 滝のをとはたえて久しくなりぬれどなこそながれてなほきこえけれ

㊼ 和泉式部 あらざらむこの世のほかの思ひ出によひとたびの逢ふこともがな

㊽ 紫式部 めぐりあひてみしやそれともわかぬまに雲がくれにし夜半の月かな

㊾ 大貳三位 ありま山ゐなのさゝ原かぜふけばいでそよ人をわすれやはする

㊿ 赤染衛門 やすらはでねなましものをさよふけてかたぶくまでの月をみしかな

法垣尾采士の如く次のあちるハさて宴さへておをても

思へ⑤藤原義孝 君かため惜をしくさりし合さ

へ分のくもの乱と思ひくふへ⑤右大将そん御母

ちハであまいて根ぬる枝のわくる海ハいのふひさしさお

とのハしは ㊸儀同三司母 志れじ乃ゆ志までかの

されバれふを乃ぎりの気ともの栞 ㊸藤原実方

乾路 のくと灸ふえやハにかきれとこしれ末せしもき

心方見ゆと思ひそ ㊹藤原道信朝臣 明ぬれバく

㊹ 中納言敦忠
 あひ見てののちの心にくらぶれば昔はものを思はざりけり

㊺ 謙徳公
 あはれともいふべき人はおもほえで身のいたづらになりぬべきかな

㊻ 曽祢好忠
 ゆらのとをわたる舟人かぢをたえゆくへも知らぬ恋の道かな

㊼ 恵慶法師
 八重葎しげれる宿のさびしきに人こそ見えね秋は来にけり

㊽ 源重之
 風をいたみ岩うつ浪のおのれのみくだけてものを思ふころかな

㊾ 大中臣能宣朝臣

あひみてのゝちの心にふくらぶれバむかしハものを相もハさ
をゝしりつゝきの松山浪こさじとハ ㊸中納言敦忠
思ひそめてク ㊷清原元輔 ちぎりきなかたみにそでを
竜まてふるこのなをハぎきちふたり人しれすこそ
もじの原ハ物や思ことく人にしられで ㊶壬生忠見
此古ひしき ㊵平兼盛 しのぶれど色に出にけり
浅茅生の小野のしの原しのぶれど何まりてちどの人
みだれちのひてし人め気のをしも多うのみ ㊴参議等

㉝ 紀友則　ひさかたのひかりのどけき春の日にしづ心なく花のちるらむ

㉞ 菅原眞風（菅家）　このたびはぬさもとりあへず手向山もみぢのにしき神のまにまに

㉟ 紀貫之　人はいさ心もしらずふるさとは花ぞむかしの香ににほひける

㊱ 春望ほうし（春道列樹）　山川に風のかけたるしがらみは流れもあへぬ紅葉なりけり

㊲ 文屋朝康　白露に風の吹きしく秋の野はつらぬきとめぬ玉ぞちりける

㊳ 右近　忘らるる身をば思はず

㉘源宗于朝臣 山里ハ冬ぞさびしさまされる人めも草もかれぬと思へむ

㉙凡河内躬恒 心あてにをらばやをらん初霜のおきまどはせる白ぎくの花

㉚壬生忠岑 有明のつれなくみえし別れより暁ばかりうきものはなし

㉛坂上是則 朝ぼらけ有明の月と見るまでによしのゝ里にふれる白雪

㉜春道列樹 山河に風のかけたるしがらみは流れもあへぬもみぢなりけり

㉒ 文屋康秀 吹くからに秋の草木のしをるればう
べ山風をわらしとらふらん ㉓大江千里 月見れば
ちぐ物こそかなしけれ 我身ひとつの秋ハいへねど
㉔ 菅家 此たびハぬさもと里あへず 手向山紅葉の
錦神のまに／＼ ㉕三條右大臣 名にしおはゞ逢坂山の
さねかづら人にしられでくる由もかな ㉖貞信公 をぐ
ら山峯のもみぢばゝむあらば今一度のみゆきまたなむ
㉗中納言兼輔 みかの原わきてながるゝいづみ川いつみきと

⑰ 在原業平朝臣
世の中にたえて桜のなかりせば春の心はのどけからまし

⑱ 藤原敏行朝臣
住の江の岸による波よるさへや夢の通ひ路人目よくらむ

⑲ 伊勢 雑
難波潟みじかき芦のふしの間も逢はでこの世を過してよとや

⑳ 元良親王
わびぬれば今はた同じ難波なるみをつくしても逢はんとぞ思ふ

㉑ 素性法師
今来んといひしばかりに長月の有明の月を待ち出でつるかな

⑪參議篁 わたの原八十嶋かけてこぎ出ぬと人には告げよあまのつり舟 ⑫僧正遍昭 天つ風雲の通ひぢ吹きとぢよをとめのすがたしばしとゞめん ⑬陽成院 つくばねの峯よりおつるみなの川恋ぞつもりて淵となりぬる ⑭河原左大臣 みちのくのしのぶもぢずり誰ゆゑにみだれそめにし我ならなくに ⑮光孝天皇 君がため春の野に出でゝ若菜つむ我が衣手に雪はふりつゝ ⑯中納言行平 立ち別れいなばの山の峯に生ふるまつとし聞かば今帰り來む

⑥中納言家持 かさゝきのわたせるはしにおくしも
の白きをみれバ夜ぞふけにける ⑦安倍仲麻呂
天乃原ふりさけみれバ春日なるみかさの山にいでし月かも ⑧喜撰法師 わが庵ハ都のたつみしかぞ
すむ世をうぢ山と人ハいふなり ⑨小野小町
花の色ハうつりにけりないたづらにわが身よにふ
るながめせしまに ⑩蝉丸 これやこの行もかへるも
別れてハしるもしらぬもあふ坂の関

① 天智天皇　秋乃田乃かりほの庵を仮に
こ我衣手は露ぞぬれつゝ
ぎてぞ長きみけしゝ白妙の衣ほすとふあまの
香具山 ③ 柿本人麻呂　あしびきの山鳥の尾
のしだり尾のながながしよをひとりかもねん
赤人　田子乃浦にうち出てみれば白妙の富士の
高ねに雪はふりつゝ ⑤ 猿丸大夫　おくやまに
もみぢふみ分けをふく鹿のこゑきく時ぞ秋はかなしき
② 持統天皇　春すぎて夏きにけらし白妙の衣ほすとふあまの
④ 山部

www.ingramcontent.com/pod-product-compliance
Lightning Source LLC
Chambersburg PA
CBHW031600170426
43196CB00032B/742